NOW PLAYING
Learning Communication Through Film

2011 INSTRUCTOR'S EDITION

Russell F. Proctor II
Northern Kentucky University

Darin Garard
Santa Barbara City College

Ronald B. Adler
Santa Barbara City College

New York   Oxford
Oxford University Press
2011

Oxford University Press, Inc., publishes works that further Oxford University's
objective of excellence in research, scholarship, and education.

Oxford   New York
Auckland   Cape Town   Dar es Salaam   Hong Kong   Karachi
Kuala Lumpur   Madrid   Melbourne   Mexico City   Nairobi
New Delhi   Shanghai   Taipei   Toronto

With offices in
Argentina   Austria   Brazil   Chile   Czech Republic   France   Greece
Guatemala   Hungary   Italy   Japan   Poland   Portugal   Singapore
South Korea   Switzerland   Thailand   Turkey   Ukraine   Vietnam

Published by Oxford University Press, Inc.
198 Madison Avenue, New York, New York 10016
http://www.oup.com

ISBN 978-0-19-979379-2

Printing number: 9 8 7 6 5 4 3 2 1

Printed in the United States of America
on acid-free paper.

CONTENTS

Section V: Additional Films with Mini-Viewing Guides 120

Section VI: References and Resources 132

Index by Communication Concepts 135

INTRODUCTION

In 1984, I was asked to teach my first course in interpersonal communication. I am embarrassed to admit that upon drafting a syllabus, I didn't have enough material to fill the semester. As a result, a search began for meaningful activities to flesh out the course. Among the people I consulted was my wife, Pam, who told me that one of the most memorable activities from her undergraduate days had been a professor's use of the movie *12 Angry Men* to teach group communication concepts. The idea seemed inspired, so I decided to adopt and adapt it by showing the film *Breaking Away* to illustrate principles of interpersonal communication.

Fast forward to now. I am still teaching interpersonal communication classes and have shown and discussed *Breaking Away* more than 75 times. I now offer an advanced interpersonal course each year in which ten feature films serve as case studies for analysis (several students from that course assisted in writing this book). Along the way there have been journal articles, convention papers, and textbook essays about feature films, identifying how they can be used in courses as diverse as interviewing, group process, communication theories, persuasion, and rhetorical criticism (and, of course, interpersonal communication). My primary compatriots in these endeavors have been Ron Adler, whose textbooks were my first teaching resources back in 1984, and Em Griffin, the professor whose film use inspired Pam.

It's a happy-ending story, but the road has not always been smooth. When I first showed *Breaking Away* in class, I somehow thought the movie would "speak for itself." As the end credits rolled, I turned on the lights and asked the class, "So, what did you learn?" They looked at me with blank expressions; a few of them ventured appraisals of the actors' performances. Clearly they had missed the boat, and so had I. Because movies are primarily an entertainment medium, viewing them as case studies for communication analysis requires forethought and direction. The goal of this book is to offer a measure of both.

Now Playing builds on the foundation of the previous iteration of this book, which was called *Communicating In Film*. Films and scenes from the previous editions have been retained and new ones have been added. This time around, there is a separate student edition of the book, containing simply the material on the films without some of the pedagogical underpinning you will see in the pages to come.

I have already acknowledged my debt to Pam, Ron, and Em, although I doubt I could thank them enough for their ideas and support. I would also like to thank the many students who have watched films with me over the years and have contributed (sometimes unknowingly) to this book. A special word of appreciation to Carl Allison, Jenny Benjamin, Adam Diebold, Laura Eisenmenger, Kathy Francis, Laura Linville, Valerie Macarie, John Renaker, Kathy Renaker (who was once Kathy Blomer—she worked on two editions of *Communication in Film*, before and after marriage!), Rosie Rock, and Leigh Ann Schroeder, all of whom graduated from the student role to become my assistants and friends on this project. I am honored and privileged to have worked with each and every one of them.

SECTION I
THE WAYS AND MEANS OF USING FEATURE FILMS

This section is included here to answer any questions instructors may have about the idea of using feature films to teach communication concepts. The central assumption of this book is that feature films are excellent instructional resources for teaching communication courses. Buying into this assumption is relatively easy; putting it into practice can be more difficult. Communication instructors typically have a variety of questions about the logistics of using feature films in their classes. This section will address some of the most common questions, using the categories of Why, What, When, Where, and How.

"Why use feature films?" has been asked and answered by various authors whose works are listed in Section VI of this book. A review of the literature suggests that feature films are valuable instructional resources because they have the potential to "(a) heighten student interest without sacrificing academic rigor, (b) utilize an existing and available resource with which students are comfortable, (c) allow classes to observe and evaluate communication processes in action, (d) expose students to worlds beyond their own, (e) provide affective as well as cognitive experiences through vicarious involvement, and (f) offer opportunities for discussion, values clarification, and personal assessment" (Proctor & Adler, 1991, p. 394).

"What are some of the most useful feature films?" is answered in Sections II and III book. 35 film scenes and 20 full-length films are discussed in detail, highlighting topics related to interpersonal communication and other communication courses. "Mini-viewing guides" of 10 more films are also provided in Section V, and other useful films are identified in the Index at the beginning of this book.

"When should feature films be used?" can be answered simply: Whenever illustrations, examples, or case studies are useful for achieving an educational goal. The length of the film excerpt should match the educational goal, as seen on the following continuum:

GOAL:	Brief Illustration		Example(s)	Case Study
LENGTH:	Film Clip	Film Scene	Multiple Scenes	Full-Length Film

(Note: Distinctions between the words "illustration" and "example" are arbitrary, and all film excerpts are "case studies" at some level. These terms are used here not as absolute categories; rather, they are employed to demonstrate differences in potential uses of feature films)

At the simplest level, a clip as short as a few seconds can be used as a brief illustration of a course concept. The idea is similar to a speaker pausing during a lecture to offer a story or incident that illustrates the point at hand. When an instructor pauses to use a film clip, the illustration becomes visual as well as verbal. Videotaped movies can be cued to the appropriate clip, then shown in class. Series of clips can also be dubbed onto a separate tape and shown in or out of class (dubbing runs the risk of infringing copyright—see the "Where" question below). DVD technology and access has advanced to the point where it will begin to dominate in instruction.

Moving to the right on the goal/length continuum, a scene or sequence of scenes can offer rich examples of course concepts. Ideally, a scene used for educational purposes should be able to "stand on its own"—that is, the communication concept should be evident in the scene even if the viewers don't have an extensive knowledge of the characters or the plotline of the movie. Section II offers a variety of communication topics depicted in "stand alone" feature film scenes.

Showing multiple scenes can move instructors closer to a case study approach without requiring as much time as the screening of a full-length movie. For example, I show several scenes from the movie *Dead Poets Society* in my Small Group Communication class to illustrate the developmental stages of Forming, Storming, Norming, and Performing. The total time of the four scenes is about 15 minutes—far more efficient than showing the entire 130-minute movie. Similarly, I show 4-5 scenes from *Mr. Holland's Opus* in my Interpersonal Communication course as examples of disconfirming/confirming communication between Mr. Holland and his son. Another approach is to show a sequence of scenes from different films. In my Small Group class, I use contrasting scenes from *Crimson Tide, 12 Angry Men,* and *Steel Magnolias* as a vehicle for discussing gender differences in leadership styles and decision-making. Instructors who want to use the multiple-scene approach can combine scenes from Section II or select/show scenes from the movies described in Section III and Section V.

Perhaps the ideal way to use feature films as case studies of human communication is to show them in their entirety rather than in clips and scenes. Viewing a full-length movie allows students to capture a sense of *process*, that elusive concept which communication professionals have been espousing since David Berlo first wrote about it in 1960. The impact of time, systemic interaction, and relational development is best illustrated when a film is seen as a whole rather than in edited parts.

Finding full-length movies for communication courses is more difficult than finding clips or scenes. It is possible, for instance, to choose and use a "good" scene from a "bad" movie, as long as it illustrates the concept well. When showing an entire film, however, the whole movie needs to have educational and illustrative value; otherwise, it is not a wise use of time. I would argue that worthwhile full-length films (educationally speaking) are relatively few and far between. Section III describes 20 movies that have been tried and tested, in their entirety, in communication courses.

The goal/length continuum can be extended farther to the right by using more than one movie in a course (perhaps by creating both in-class and out-of-class assignments). The ultimate extension of the continuum would be an entire course devoted to analyzing feature films as case studies.

"Where should feature films be used?" is a question whose answer is best determined by the educational objectives of the instructor and the amount of class time available. Bringing film into the classroom—in clips, scenes, or entire movies—allows students and instructors to share the feature film experience and discuss it while it is fresh. In my experience, showing a full-length movie during the final week of class is an excellent way to wrap up a course. The in-class viewing provides a bonding experience for the students, an excellent vehicle for reviewing course concepts, and a much-appreciated break from end-of-the-term stresses and strains.

For many instructors, however, in-class screenings do not fit their schedules or goals. In such cases, out-of-class assignments can be used. There are many ways to use movies outside the classroom: Copies of selected movies can be put on reserve in the school library; students can be asked to rent and watch a movie of their choice from a list compiled by the instructor; groups can be assigned to choose and watch a movie at the location of their choice; videotapes of edited clips can be viewed in campus media centers.

Some of these options (particularly those involving dubbed film clips) lead to the question of copyright infringement. Copyright law seems to favor in-class use of lawfully made copies of feature films. Title 17, Section 110 (1) of the United States Code permits:

> Performance or display of a work by instructors or pupils in the course of face-to-face teaching activities of a nonprofit educational institution, in a classroom or similar place devoted to instruction, unless, in the case of a motion picture or other audiovisual work, the performance, or the display of individual images, is given by means of a copy that was not lawfully made under this title, and that the person responsible for the performance knew or had reason to believe was not lawfully made.

It is beyond the scope of this book to interpret copyright law (see Section VI for references related to copyright, particularly Patterson & Lindberg, 1991; Speere & Parsons, 1995; Vicek, 1992). As a rule of thumb, instructors should abide by the spirit of the copyright law—in other words, they should use copyrighted material for nonprofit, educational purposes and should not use illegal copies that provide no compensation for the artists and/or producers.

"How should feature films be used?" is perhaps the most pressing question asked by communication instructors. A movie does not "speak for itself"; it becomes an educational resource only when instructors offer guidance for viewing and analyzing the film. Toward that end, it is not wise to show a movie or a clip, then turn on the lights and ask, "So, what do you think?" (I learned this the hard way!). Teachers and students need direction and guidance for turning entertainment media into instructional tools.

The primary method for providing direction and guidance is the use of discussion questions. Discussion questions can be employed in a variety of ways, depending upon the sophistication of the students and the goals of the instructor:

- Instructor poses questions and offers answers: For those who want to provide a high degree of direction, this approach essentially involves the instructor offering a post-viewing analysis of a movie. This approach is best suited for large-lecture classes where interaction would be difficult, or for novice audiences who are being taught how to analyze films.

- Instructor poses questions, students offer answers: For those who want to provide a moderate degree of direction, this approach involves instructors guiding students to focus on particular communication concepts. Questions posed in advance of the screening (or at pause points during the screening) provide more direction than questions posed after the screening. Students can offer their answers in written assignments, class discussions, or both. Examples of viewing guides for this approach can be found in Section IV.

- Students pose questions and offer answers: For those who want students to direct their own learning, this approach puts the ball in the students' court. A modicum of instructor direction can be provided by assigning readings in conjunction with movies; these readings can give students ideas for issues they might want to explore. Questions can be asked and answered in written assignments, class discussions, or both. This approach is best suited for mature classes in which discussion (and occasionally debate) is desired and encouraged. An example of a prep form for this approach can be found in Section IV on p. 72.

Discussion questions are provided for all entries in Sections II and III. The questions are not the only ones that can or should be asked, nor are the answers (samples are provided for the films in Section III) the "right" way to respond to the questions. They are offered simply as examples of how these scenes and movies might be used in instructional settings.

This section is a primer on ways and means of using feature films to teach communication courses. If readers have other instructional ideas, methods, or resources, please share them with your feature film colleagues through letters, e-mail, papers, and articles.

SECTION II
FEATURE FILM SCENES

Each of the entries in this section is a "stand alone" scene that illustrates communication concepts (with a strong focus on interpersonal communication). The scenes are listed below in alphabetical order; they are also arranged by category in the index at the end of the book. The time locations of the scenes are measured from the opening moment of the movie, just after the display of the film company (in other words, don't begin counting on your timer until all the previews on the video are finished).

Film: *Almost Famous*
Year: 2000
Central Concept: Self-Disclosure
Related Concepts: Identity Management, Group Communication
Approximate Scene Location: 96 minutes into the 122-minute movie
Approximate Scene Length: 4 minutes
Opening Line: Brief shot of plane flying through storm (no dialogue)
Closing Line: "Thank God we're all alive. We're going to make it!" (To capture facial expressions of the passengers after they realize they will survive, don't cut until scene ends, about 10 seconds after last line of dialogue.)

Scene Description: A 1970s rock band is on tour when its plane is caught in a violent storm. The prospect of imminent death moves several members of the group and its entourage to reveal facts and feelings they had previously kept to themselves. Some of the self-disclosing messages are positive; others are upsetting and disruptive. The scene offers a good foundation for exploring several dimensions of self-revelation: reasons for opening up, the conditions under which disclosure is likely to occur, and the risks and benefits of candor. (Note: the scene contains language that may offend some viewers.)

Discussion Questions:
1. Place the self-disclosures offered in this scene on a continuum, ranging from "appropriate under most conditions" to "inappropriate under most conditions." Describe the conditions under which the disclosures might be appropriate or inappropriate.
2. Which members of the group have been engaging in high levels of identity management with the others? What will happen to the management of their identities now that they've made these revelations?
3. Describe the following group communication concepts at work in this scene: ripple effect, conformity, openness, and boundaries.
4. Have you ever made a self-disclosure in a group of people that you later regretted? Discuss why you made the disclosure and how you managed your identity in later interactions with those people.

Film: *Click*
Year: 2006
Central Concept: Intercultural Incompetence
Related Concepts: Interpersonal Communication at Work, Coercive Power
Approximate Scene Location: 3 minutes into the 107-minute movie
Approximate Scene Length: 4 minutes
Opening Line: "Hmmm, well the interesting thing…"
Closing Line: "I'm just messing with you."

Scene Description: Workaholic architect Michael Newman is trying to earn a partnership in the firm headed by John Ammer. Ammer is arrogant, disrespectful, and insensitive in his interactions with clients and his employees, as evidenced by this scene. This scene could start a provocative discussion about intercultural and communicative competence, respect, and power in relationships.

Discussion Questions:
1. How do Ammer and Newman exhibit intercultural incompetence in their meeting with their Middle Eastern clients?
2. How could they enhance their intercultural competence?
3. Describe the dimensions of the workplace culture Ammer has created, evidenced by the exchanges between Ammer and Newman.
4. How does Ammer exercise coercive power in their relationship?

Film: *Clueless*
Year: 1995
Central Concept: Language
Related Concepts: Culture, Communication Competence, Public Speaking
Approximate Scene Location: 30 seconds into the 97-minute film
Approximate Scene Length: 4 minutes
Opening Line: "Did I show you the lumped-out jeep daddy got me?"
Closing Line: "If she doesn't do the assignment, I can't do mine."

Scene Description: Cher and her friends live in their own "contempo-casual" culture and speak their own language (depicted throughout this scene with words such as "jeepin," "outie," and "buggin'"). Their linguistic code gives them a sense of shared identity and excludes those who are not in their group. Near the end of the scene, Cher uses her group's jargon in a public speaking context, and her speech is not successful, demonstrating that language which is appropriate for an informal context is not appropriate for a formal one.

Discussion Questions:
1. Identify words/terms used by Cher and her friends that are unique to their culture. Which words/terms were not familiar to you?
2. Why do teenagers create new words and/or give old words new meanings?
3. Is it appropriate to use slang and jargon in public speeches?
4. Discuss this scene in terms of interpersonal, intercultural, and public speaking competence.

Film: *Dead Man Walking*
Year: 1996
Central Concept: Perception (Stereotyping and Prejudice)
Related Concepts: Communication Climate, Listening, Language
Approximate Scene Location: 40 minutes into the 120-minute film
Approximate Scene Length: 3 minutes
Opening Line: "Rain, rain, rain . . . that's a bad sign." (in the middle of a prison cell discussion)
Closing Line: "Can we talk about something else?"

Scene Description: This scene is an interpersonal communication tour de force. Helen Prejean is a nun who befriends death-row prisoner Matthew Poncelet prior to his execution. She confronts Poncelet about his prejudices regarding African-Americans. Poncelet's perceptions and language are filled with stereotypes and generalizations about "niggers" and "coloreds." Prejean's questions and responses require him to think (which he doesn't seem to want to do) about inaccuracies in his generalizations. Some of her comments are loaded and get defensive reactions; most are reflective and allow Poncelet to hear his prejudices in another voice. When Prejean's probing digs too deep (she gets him to realize "it's lazy people you don't like," not blacks), Poncelet asks Prejean to change the subject—which she agrees to do. This scene is worthy of line-by-line analysis.

Discussion Questions:
1. What factors influenced Poncelet's perceptions, prejudices, and stereotypes?
2. What listening skills does Prejean use to draw information from Poncelet? How do these skills get/keep Poncelet talking and thinking?
3. What questions/statements by Prejean prompt a defensive response from Poncelet?
4. Discuss the use of responsible and irresponsible language in the scene and its relationship to communication climate.

Film: *Election*
Year: 1999
Central Concept: Persuasion
Related Concept: Public Speaking
Approximate Scene Location: 36 minutes into the 103-minute film
Approximate Scene Length: 5 minutes
Opening Line: "We'll move on now to the presidential race."
Closing Line: "Don't vote at all!"

Scene Description: Three candidates are running for student government president at Carver High School: Tracy, Paul, and Tammy. Each is required to give a brief speech at a student assembly. Tracy's presentation is memorized, well constructed, and delivered with precision and flair (and a dose of overconfidence, which generates crude catcalls from students who think she is stuck up). Paul, a popular athlete, reads his speech directly from his notecards. While his content is solid, he has little or no eye contact, facial expression, or vocal variety—and the students don't know how to respond (they are prompted to applaud by a teacher). Tammy, Paul's sister, thinks that student government is a joke; she is running for election to spite her brother and his girlfriend. She speaks extemporaneously and with passion about the "pathetic" election process and encourages people to either vote for her or not vote at all. She gets a rousing response.

Discussion Questions:
1. Identify the strengths and weaknesses of each of the candidates' speeches.
2. Evaluate the persuasive appeals of each candidate in terms of logos, pathos, and ethos.
3. Which candidate would get your vote—and why?

Film: *Fantastic Mr. Fox*
Year: 2009
Central Concept: Leadership
Related Concepts: Group Cohesiveness, Power in Groups
Approximate Scene Location: 58 minutes into the 87-minute film
Approximate Scene Length: 3 minutes
Opening Line: "My suicide mission has been canceled."
Closing Line: "I doubt they had opossums in ancient Rome."

Scene Description: *Fantastic Mr. Fox* is director Wes Craven's interpretation of the classic Roald Dahl novel, by the same name. Filmed in stop-motion animation, the plot revolves around the adventures of Mr. Fox, a wild fox stuck in the mundane routines of raising and supporting his family. Unable to contain his natural instincts, Fox steals food from the local farmers until he pushes them too far, and an all-out war on animals ensues. After their homes are destroyed and his nephew taken hostage, Fox has to find a way to save his family and friends from the farmers' wrath. In this scene, Fox needs to rally support for his new plan to stop the farmers and rescue his nephew. He resumes his toast to his companions, but this time Fox points out their strengths as individuals and as a team. Reminding them of their unique talents and skills, Fox successfully creates group cohesion and motivates his followers to support his plan.

Discussion Questions:
1. Which factors (e.g., shared goals, perceived threats, etc.) does Mr. Fox rely on to motivate his group followers and create cohesiveness? Identify and provide examples.
2. Identify which type (or types) of power in groups that Fox demonstrates. How effective would his style be in different small group contexts (e.g., a family conflict or business meeting)? Why?
3. Which theory of leadership effectiveness (Trait, Style, or Situational) best exemplifies Mr. Fox's approach? Explain your choice.
4. Pick one example from your life when you were a follower in a small group, such as a sports team, summer camp, or work group. How did your leader attempt to create group cohesiveness? What types of power did your leader exercise? Which leadership approach was taken?
5. Pick a different example from your life when you were the leader in a small group, again such as a sports team, summer camp, or work group. How did you attempt to create group cohesiveness? What types of power did you exercise? Which leadership approach did you take?

Film: *Finding Forrester*
Year: 2000
Central Concept: Perception (Stereotyping)
Related Concepts: Culture, Identity Management
Approximate Scene Location: 18 minutes into the 136-minute film
Approximate Scene Length: 1 minute
Opening Line: "I'm not going to do anything to your car, man."
Closing Line: "No problem, man"

Scene Description: Jamal is an African-American teenager whose intelligence earns him a full scholarship to a prestigious, all-white prep school. He lives, however, in a tough, all-black neighborhood—so he often feels caught between two cultures. In this scene, a white man parks a sporty BMW in Jamal's neighborhood. When Jamal approaches the car, he perceives the driver reacting defensively. The two men have a tense conversation in which Jamal, by demonstrating his knowledge about the BMW company, attempts to disprove any stereotypes the driver might have about him.

Discussion Questions:
1. Describe how and why both the driver and Jamal engage in stereotyping at the outset of this scene. What nonverbal and verbal cues are involved?
2. Explain the role of selection, organization, and interpretation in the perceptions these two men hold of each other. Do their perceptions change as a result of their conversation? If so, how and why?
3. Discuss how the driver and Jamal engage in identity management throughout this scene. Use three words to describe the identity that each man tries to present.

Film: *Ghost Town*
Year: 2008
Central Concept: Avoidance of Communication
Related Concepts: Unwillingness to Communicate, Listening, Self-Disclosure
Approximate Scene Location: 5 minutes into the 102-minute film
Approximate Scene Length: 2 minutes
Opening Line: "Okay, go ahead and spit."
Closing Line: "So cute"

Scene Description: Bertram Pincus would be happy if other people simply left him alone. Paraphrasing John Donne he proclaims "*This* man is an island." Although Bertram enjoys the comfortable routine of his job as a dentist, he cannot stand the scripted conversations with his patients and coworkers. To make his life even worse, a complication during a medical procedure leaves Bertram with an unusual ability: he can now communicate with dead people as well as the living. In this scene, Bertram displays his style of avoiding communication with others. It works well to illustrate both verbal and nonverbal cues of avoidance, which students should easily identify. Moreover, this scene will provide a springboard to students' personal examples of communication avoidance.

Discussion Questions:
1. Identify both verbal and nonverbal cues that illustrate how Bertram attempts to avoid communication with others.
2. Even though Bertram obviously hears other people, how could his style of communication be considered ineffective listening? Which type of ineffective listening is it? Please explain.
3. Consider your own personal experiences with trying to avoid communicating with others. What were the reasons you were unwilling to communicate? What cues (both verbal and nonverbal) did you exhibit to illustrate your unwillingness? How did the other person respond?
4. Although this scene is entirely face-to-face, how has technology (e.g., cell phones, computers, etc.) changed the ways we avoid communication with others? Is avoidance easier or more difficult now because of technology?

Film: *Grease*
Year: 1978
Central Concept: Identity Management
Related Concepts: Nonverbal, Communication Competence
Approximate Scene Location: 22 minutes into the 110-minute movie
Approximate Scene Length: 2 minutes
Opening Line: "Hey, Sandy, we've got a surprise for you."
Closing Line: "Sandy, men are rats."

Scene Description: Sandy and Danny spent the summer in a blissful romance (the subject of the hit song, "Summer Nights"). When they parted ways at the end of the season, they thought they would never see each other again. Sandy's family moves, however, she ends up attending Rydell High. When she tells her new friends about her summer fling with a guy named Danny, they figure out that it's the same Danny who attends Rydell—and they set them up for a surprise "re-meeting." When Danny and Sandy first see each other, their faces and voices fill with delight. Quickly, however, Danny realizes he is in front of his hood buddies—and he changes his persona to be tough and cool rather than sensitive and sweet. Sandy is bewildered and devastated that the Danny she knew over the summer is so dramatically different from the Danny at Rydell High.

Discussion Questions:
1. Discuss this scene in terms of identity management. Why does Danny's self-presentation change so dramatically, while Sandy's does not?
2. Discuss the nonverbal messages Danny sends in this scene. When and how does he (and doesn't he) "leak" information about how he really feels?
3. Would you assess Danny as being "phony" or "communicatively competent" in this scene? What is the line of difference between the two? Explain your answer with concepts from the textbook.
4. Have you ever been in a similar situation where you felt "caught" between people you know from very different roles and contexts? How did you handle it?

Film: *Gung Ho*
Year: 1986
Central Concept: Culture
Related Concept: Communication Competence, Public Speaking
Approximate Scene Location: 8 minutes into the 110-minute film
Approximate Scene Length: 4 minutes
Opening Line: "Hi, fellas" (after entering the building with screen in hand)
Closing Line: "C'mon . . . c'mon" (with head in hands)

Scene Description: A scene reminiscent of *The Ugly American*: Hunt Stevenson goes to Japan in an attempt to lure Assan Motors to bring their business to his hometown of Hadleyville. His pitch to the Assan executives is an excellent example of what *not* to do. Clearly, Stevenson has not analyzed his audience or the setting (e.g., he lugs a projector screen to the session, not realizing that the room in which he is presenting is very high-tech). Moreover, he makes comments that are culturally insensitive (e.g., references to World War II) and interpersonally offensive (e.g., coarse references to women and underwear). The scene is very funny, but it is also uncomfortable.

Discussion Questions:
1. In what ways does Hunt Stevenson exhibit intercultural incompetence?
2. In what ways does Stevenson demonstrate that he has not analyzed his audience/setting?
3. How could Stevenson have made this pitch more effectively?

Film: *He's Just Not That Into You*
Year: 2009
Central Concept: Technology
Related Concepts: Computer-Mediated Communication, Relational Stages, Relational Maintenance
Approximate Scene Location: 67 minutes into the 129-minute film
Approximate Scene Length: 2 minutes
Opening Line: "He's leaving his wife for me!"
Closing Line: "Yeah…I felt like we connected."

Scene Description: Inspired by a pop culture book with the same name, *He's Just Not That Into You* dispenses romantic advice to its hopelessly confused female cast. Stacked with stereotypes, the entire film is intended to be a lesson on reading subtle verbal and nonverbal cues of potential romantic partners – to determine if he really is "into you." In this scene, Mary is expressing her frustration with today's technologically-driven dating culture. Exasperated, Mary tells her girlfriend Anna how she longs for simpler times when technology was less ubiquitous and dating was a face-to-face experience.

9

Discussion Questions:

1. Explain why Mary is so upset. Does she have a legitimate complaint? Why or why not?
2. Identify the types of technologies (e.g., email, cell phones, social networking sites) you utilize to *initiate* romantic relationships. Which medium is the most effective? Why? Which mediums are more effective for *maintaining* romantic relationships?
3. Describe a personal example when you experienced *benefits* from using technology instead of face-to-face communication. What is gained by using these technologies?
4. Likewise, describe a personal example when you felt *restricted* by using technology instead of face-to-face communication. What is lost by using these technologies?

Film: *Hitch*
Year: 2005
Central Concept: Interpersonal Relationships
Related Concepts: Nonverbal, Gender Influence on Relationships
Approximate Scene Location: 43 minutes into the 118-minute movie
Approximate Scene Length: 9 minutes
Opening Line: "Keep it simple, like we practiced."
Closing Line: "When they're good"

Scene Description: In *Hitch*, Alex "Hitch" Hitchens is a New York date doctor who teaches men how to romance the women of their dreams. Hitch's latest client is Albert Brennaman, a nerdy financial consultant who needs to develop a more macho communication style to win the heart of wealthy and beautiful Allegra Cole. The scene provides many examples of incompetent interactions and dating behaviors to discuss.

Discussion Questions:

1. How, specifically, does Hitch encourage Albert to change his verbal communication when interacting with Allegra?
2. Which nonverbal behaviors does Hitch coach Albert to change, and why?
3. What bits of advice does Hitch offer Albert to increase his attractiveness? Which tips do you believe are and are not sound?

Film: *I Love You, Man*
Year: 2009
Central Concept: Terminating Relationships
Related Concepts: Conflict, Friendship Rules, Relational Maintenance
Approximate Scene Location: 82 minutes into the 105-minute film
Approximate Scene Length: 3 minutes
Opening Line: "Yeah…it's open"
Closing Line: "Bye, Anwar."

Scene Description: As the title may suggest, *I Love You, Man* focuses on the male friendship – or "bromance" – between Peter and Sydney. Peter is a newly engaged realtor living in Los Angeles. When his fiancée asks him who his best man will be at their wedding, Peter suddenly realizes that he does not have any male friends. At a chance encounter during a house showing, Peter meets Sydney, a free-spirited individual also looking for friendship. The remainder of the film follows the stages of Peter and Sydney's relationship, complete with escalating, bonding, and deteriorating. In this scene, Peter confronts Sydney about several recent billboards around Los Angeles baring his likeness. Conflict ensues, Peter and Sydney 'break-up' and end their friendship. The scene works as an effective illustration of Knapp's terminating stage, along with how individuals establish and violate friendship rules.

Discussion Questions:
1. Explain how this scene demonstrates Knapp's terminating stage of relational deterioration.
2. Are there certain 'rules' to follow when ending friendships? Identify three rules you follow.
3. Are there certain 'rules' to follow for ending romantic relationships? Identify three rules you follow.
4. Describe a personal example when you ended a friendship. Was the termination a gradual withdrawal from your friend, or was it a sudden ending of the relationship?
5. In order to avoid reaching the terminating stage, what are strategies you use to maintain a friendship? Identify three relational maintenance strategies you use to keep your friendships from terminating.

Film: *The Invention of Lying*
Year: 2009
Central Concept: Self-Disclosure
Related Concepts: Honesty, Uncertainty Reduction, Identity Management, Saving Face
Approximate Scene Location: 4 minutes into the 99-minute film
Approximate Scene Length: 3 minutes
Opening Line: "This is not as nice as I remember it."
Closing Line: "How is your mom? Alright? Great!"

Scene Description: *The Invention of Lying* is a fictional tale about a world where no one can lie, not even a fib or a white lie – except one man. Mark Bellison discovers his unique gift and sets out to solve all of the world's problems, become rich and famous, and win the heart of the woman he loves. Predictably, Mark's plans do not always turn out the way he envisioned them. Perhaps the film would be more aptly titled *Too Much Self-Disclosure*, since the storyline really isn't so much about lying. Instead, it's more about the inability to refrain from verbalizing your every thought. The characters say whatever pops into their heads, no matter the context, and apparently without any negative outcomes – indeed a fictional tale. In this scene, Mark is on a date with Anna McDoogles. It is a typical first-date scenario for both characters, complete with feelings of uncertainty and anxiety about each other. Well, it's typical except for one small detail: they cannot control their self-disclosure. Pay special attention to the topics that are discussed, along with their atypical answers. In a world where honesty isn't simply the best policy – it's the only policy – a little self-disclosure can go a very long way.

Discussion Questions:
1. Using the terms depth, breadth, and reciprocity of self-disclosure, how is their first date typical of most first dates? How is it different from most first dates?
2. Consider your own past experiences on first dates. What topics do you typically discuss? Are these topics goal-oriented (e.g., to reduce uncertainty, to secure a second date, etc.)? In what ways?
3. Compare and contrast the characters' public and private selves. How are they managing their identity through communication?
4. Describe a situation when you were aware of your different selves, and you felt the need to manage your identity. Were you successful?
5. Is honesty always the best policy? Describe a situation when saving someone's face, without being completely honest, was the best choice – the choice of a competent communicator.

Film: *Invictus*
Year: 2009
Central Concept: Persuasive Speaking
Related Concepts: Credibility, Audience Analysis, Leadership and Power
Approximate Scene Location: 27 minutes into the 134-minute film
Approximate Scene Length: 8 minutes
Opening Line: "And now for the next item on our agenda."
Closing Line: "A luxury. We only needed one more yes than no."

Scene Description: *Invictus* is the real-life story about then South African President Nelson Mandela, and his plan to use rugby to unite his country following the demise of apartheid. Set in 1994-1995, newly elected President Mandela is struggling to move his nation forward, both politically and economically, in the eyes of the world. While attending a rugby match of the Springboks, the country's national rugby team, Mandela notices that blacks actually cheer against their home team – for them a longstanding symbol of racism and hatred – while Afrikaners (whites) root for the Springboks. Knowing that South Africa would host the Rugby World Cup in one year, Mandela enlists the aid of the Springbok's captain to promote the sport as a symbol of unity and nationalism, instead of hatred and violence. In this scene, Mandela must persuade South Africa's National Sports Council (the governing body in charge of the country's sports) not to change the Springbok team's name and colors. The National Sports Council, like most of the country's black citizens, views the Springboks as a symbol of apartheid. Learning that the Council has voted to dismantle the Springboks, Mandela rushes to their meeting in an attempt to persuade them otherwise. Facing a hostile audience, Mandela uses his credibility and audience analysis to successfully, by a narrow margin, convince the Council of his viewpoint.

Discussion Questions:
1. Using propositions, outcomes, and directness, identify the type of persuasive speech Mandela gives.
2. How does Mandela adapt to his audience (the National Sports Council)? What strategies does he use to appeal to this target audience?
3. Recall a time when you gave a speech to persuade, even an informal talk to a group. What strategies did you use to adapt to your audience? Were you successful? If not, how could you have increased your success through improved audience analysis?
4. Consider Mandela's credibility as a speaker. What characteristics about him increase the audience's perception of his credibility? How does Mandela use these characteristics in his speech?
5. Think back to a moment when you were in the audience for a persuasive speech. Did you consider the speaker to be credible? Why? If not, what could the speaker have done to increase your perceptions of his or her credibility?
6. Identify the types of power Mandela uses to influence the National Sports Council. How are power and credibility necessarily interwoven? Is it possible to separate them?

Film: *The Joy Luck Club*
Year: 1993
Central Concept: Culture
Related Concept: Communication Competence
Approximate Scene Location: 43 minutes into the 138-minute film
Approximate Scene Length: 4 minutes
Opening Line: "The next week I brought Rich to Mom's birthday dinner" (Waverly's voice)
Closing Line: "All this needs is a little soy sauce"

Scene Description: Waverly, a Chinese-American woman, brings her Anglo-American boyfriend Rich home for a dinner cooked by her Chinese mother, Lindo. Rich unknowingly insults Waverly's family when he fails to follow the rules of Chinese dining. For instance, he shocks everyone at the table by taking a large first serving of the entree. As Waverly explains in her narration, it is customary in Chinese culture to take only a small spoonful of a dish until everyone else has had some. Rich's biggest mistake is when he misunderstands Lindo's description of her prized entree. Lindo says, "This dish no good. Too salty." Rich decodes the message literally, not paying attention to Lindo's nonverbal cues. The family knows that when Lindo insults her cooking, it means she is pleased with it. The implicit rule is to eat some, then compliment it profusely. Instead, Rich floods the prized dish with soy sauce and assures Lindo that it is not beyond repair.

Discussion Questions:
1. What differences between American and Chinese cultures are depicted in this scene? Use terms from lecture and text in your analysis.
2. What could Rich have done to enhance his intercultural competence?

Film: *License to Wed*
Year: 2007
Central Concept: Listening
Related Concepts: Empathic Listening, Social Support Messages, Listening and Gender
Approximate Scene Location: 71 minutes into the 91-minute film
Approximate Scene Length: 2 minutes
Opening Line: "It wasn't supposed to be like this."
Closing Line: "I don't need anyone telling me!"

Scene Description: Ben Murphy and Sadie Jones are head-over-heels in love with each other. Ben proposes to Sadie, she accepts, and the happy couple begins planning their wedding. In order to be married at the church of Sadie's dreams, however, they learn that they must participate in a prenuptial course taught by the eccentric Reverend Frank. The Reverend's intense, and intrusive, course creates conflict between Ben and Sadie, resulting in their break-up and cancellation of the wedding. In this scene Ben is talking to his best friend, Joel, seeking his support and advice about how to get Sadie back. Unfortunately for Ben, Joel is an incompetent listener. In an otherwise forgettable film, this scene illustrates well how most typical forms of social support are ineffective.

Discussion Questions:
1. How would you label and describe Joel's style of listening? Use examples from their dialogue to justify your answer.
2. Clearly Joel's listening style is not working for Ben. What could Joel have said to Ben that would have been more competent? Create and role-play a new dialogue between Ben and Joel that incorporates your suggestions.
3. This scene supports the gender stereotype that men tend to respond to others' problems by giving advice. What has been your experience with listening style differences because of gender?
4. Recall a recent episode when you were seeking social support from someone. Describe what was said during the conversation and your perception of the outcome, whether it was positive or negative.

Film: *Love Actually*
Year: 2003
Central Concepts: Nonverbal (Deception and Leakage)
Related Concepts: Ethics of Deception
Approximate Scene Location: 28 minutes into the 135-minute film
Approximate Scene Length: 1 minute, 30 seconds
Opening Line: "So, what's the problem?"
Closing Line: "You're right. Total agony"

Scene Description: Daniel is very worried about his 11-year-old stepson, Sam. Sam's mother died recently, and he has spent nearly all his time alone in his room, leading Daniel to wonder if Sam is using drugs. In this scene, Daniel learns that Sam's "problem" is that he is in love. Daniel is delighted that drugs are not the issue, but he quickly realizes that Sam is taking this puppy love very seriously—and as a result, Daniel attempts to mask the relief and elation he is feeling.

Discussion Questions:
1. Daniel is trying to hide his happiness from Sam, but he is having a hard time doing it. What indications of leakage (showing his true feelings) do you see in Daniel?
2. Why do you think Daniel feels the need to hide his feelings of joy from Sam?
3. Daniel is trying to lie about his feelings. Do you think it's wrong for Daniel to deceive Sam in this manner? Explain your answer.

Film: *Mean Girls*
Year: 2004
Central Concept: Communication Climate
Related Concepts: Conflict, Empathy
Approximate Scene Location: 70 minutes into the 96-minute film
Approximate Scene Length: 5 minutes, 30 seconds
Opening Line: "Ms. Norbury, you're a successful, caring, intelligent, graceful young woman."
Closing Line: "Suck on that. Aye yie yie yie!" (as she falls backward to be caught by the other girls)

Scene Description: The girls of the junior class at North Shore High School are constantly in conflict. The disagreements, disconfirmation, and backstabbing (including mean evaluations written in a scrapbook called a "Burn Book") reach a breaking point when the fighting nearly leads to a riot. In response, the school principal calls all the junior girls to the gym where one of the school's teachers, Ms. Norbury, leads them in an "attitude makeover."

Discussion Questions:
1. What is Ms. Norbury's purpose with the two exercises she does where the girls close their eyes? How does it enhance the communication climate and empathy level among the girls?
2. Ms. Norbury says, "You all have got to stop calling each other sluts and whores. It just makes it okay for guys to call you sluts and whores." Do you agree with her assessment? Discuss in terms of course concepts.
3. What style(s) of conflict management does Ms. Norbury use? Is the approach effective in this situation? Discuss how well this approach would (or wouldn't) work in other conflict situations.

Film: *Medicine for Melancholy*
Year: 2009
Central Concept: Self-Concept
Related Concepts: Perception, Culture, Stereotyping
Approximate Scene Location: 64 minutes into the 88-minute film
Approximate Scene Length: 5 minutes
Opening Line: "A lot of second-hand smoke"
Closing Line: "I don't wanna talk anymore."

Scene Description: Understated yet thought provoking, *Medicine for Melancholy* is a slice-of-life story. Set in San Francisco, the film follows the awkward and uncertain moments of two twenty-somethings (Micah and Jo) after their one night stand. Not only do the characters struggle with defining their relationship, they each wrestle with definitions of their identity. In this scene, Micah and Jo are debating the meaning of being African-American while living in predominately-white San Francisco. Rather pointedly, Micah defines himself as "a black man," while Jo sees herself as more than any one quality. The scene encourages us to contemplate our own identity and worldview, and to question how we see ourselves through the eyes of others.

Discussion Questions:
1. When meeting someone for the first time (face-to-face), what do you typically notice about the other person? What judgments do you make? How does your perception, then, influence your communication with this person?
2. Describe how Micah sees himself, and how Jo sees herself. Speculate how and why each person formed their own worldviews.
3. Take a few minutes and write down ten different characteristics of your self-concept – who you think you are. After you have completed your list, explain how and why you define yourself this way. What experiences shaped your self-concept?
4. Do you think it is possible to define yourself by one quality (e.g., race or gender or class)? Describe a moment from your life when someone else defined you by only one quality, and treated you in a way that fulfilled that stereotype.

Film: *Nothing Like the Holidays*
Year: 2008
Central Concept: Family Communication
Related Concepts: Punctuation, Conflict, Identity Management
Approximate Scene Location: 47 minutes into the 98-minute film
Approximate Scene Length: 5 minutes
Opening Line: "Hey Father Torres, good to see you."
Closing Line: "Jesse!"

Scene Description: A Puerto Rican family with a long history in their Chicago neighborhood gathers for their annual Christmas get-together. Normally, the Rodriguez family participates in traditional rituals signifying the season – going to church, caroling, and parades. The siblings, however, soon realize that all is not well between their parents, and this holiday may be their last together as a family. In this scene, the eldest son (Mauricio) has taken it upon himself to organize a family intervention, hoping to prevent his parent's divorce. To her surprise, Anna (the family matriarch) comes home to find her three children, husband, and Father Torres sitting around the dinner table. The scene works well to illustrate family dynamics, as the discussion quickly shifts from the parents' divorce to the siblings' perceptions of their family roles.

Discussion Questions:
1. How would you describe this family system? What are the roles each family member plays? Are they symmetrical or complementary to each other?
2. Consider your own family system for a moment. What roles do you and other family members play? Would you consider your relationship with other members to be symmetrical or complementary?
3. Each member of the Rodriguez family appears to be talking from their own perspective, not the perspective of others. Choose two characters and explain their conflict by identifying differences in punctuation.
4. How does the mother manage her identity around Father Torres? Compare her perceived self with her presenting self.

Film: *Office Space* (Scene 1)
Year: 1999
Central Concept: Communication Climate
Related Concepts: Listening, Emotions, Nonverbal
Approximate Scene Location: 3 minutes into the 88-minute film
Approximate Scene Length: 5 minutes
Opening Line: Peter walking through the office door as the film credits roll
Closing Line: "Yes, I have the memo!"

Scene Description: From the minute Peter walks in the office on Monday morning at Initech, it is clear that he hates his mundane, dehumanizing job. One of the reasons is the way he is treated by his boss, Lumbergh, who approaches him and asks, "What's happening?" It is a counterfeit question because Lumbergh really doesn't want to know how Peter is doing, nor is he looking for any small talk about the weekend. Instead, he wants to confront Peter about a small mistake in his TPS report. He delivers a patronizing monologue to Peter in a calm, syrupy tone of voice—and shows no interest in Peter's explanation of the problem. After Lumbergh walks away, two other managers confront Peter about the same problem, using the same patronizing tone and lack of listening skills.

Discussion Questions:
1. Describe the communication climate between Peter and his managers. What factors from Gibb's climate model are evident in their interactions?
2. Discuss the managers' listening responses, both verbal and nonverbal, using terms from your textbook.
3. The managers in this scene use calm voices and avoid angry words, yet Peter still feels like he is being "yelled at." Explain how and why this is the case. How might the bosses have communicated their messages more effectively?
4. Watch this scene with the volume turned off. Attempt to describe what the characters are thinking and feeling simply by monitoring their nonverbal cues.

Film: *Office Space* (Scene 2)
Year: 1999
Central Concept: Communication Climate
Related Concepts: Language, Listening, Perception
Approximate Scene Location: 37 minutes into the 88-minute film
Approximate Scene Length: 1 minute
Opening Line: "Joanna, can I talk to you for a minute?"
Closing Line: "Some people choose to wear more; you do want to express yourself, don't you?"

Scene Description: Joanna is a waitress at Chotchkie's, a restaurant in the mold of Friday's and Bennigan's. Her manager is less than happy with her performance and calls her aside for a pep talk.

Unfortunately, he creates a defensive communication climate by sending messages that are, to use Gibb's terms, evaluative, controlling, strategic, neutral, and superior. The manager is ambiguous and indirect as he talks to Joanna about her "flair" (a euphemism meant to describe the environment of fun at Chotchkie's, but something he measures by the number of buttons on her uniform). He also sends her negative nonverbal messages through a patronizing tone of voice and by rolling his eyes. Instead of describing what he wants from her, he asks impersonal and counterfeit questions such as, "What do you think of a person that only does the bare minimum?" and "Some people choose to wear more [flair buttons]; you do want to express yourself, don't you?"

Discussion Questions:
1. What is the communication climate between Joanna and her manager? What verbal and nonverbal messages are factors in the creating that climate?
2. Give examples of how the manager's language illustrates the concepts of vagueness, abstraction, and euphemisms. Describe how he could convey his concerns more precisely, concretely, and constructively.
3. Discuss how the manager uses counterfeit questioning in his listening responses. How could he have asked the same questions more sincerely?
4. Joanna attempts to use perception checking to clarify her manager's request. What effect does this have on their communication, and why?

Film: *One True Thing*
Year: 1998
Central Concept: Family Communication
Related Concept: Communication Climate
Approximate Scene Location: 29 minutes into the 127-minute film
Approximate Scene Length: 2 minutes, 30 seconds
Opening Line: "I'm glad you're home."
Closing Line: "Thanks for taking care of this."

Scene Description: Freelance writer Ellen Gulden grew up idolizing her father George, a self-important professor and literary critic. Ellen comes home for a surprise birthday party honoring George and soon learns that her mother is stricken with cancer. This scene takes place in George's study, where he invites Ellen to write the introduction to a volume of his collected essays. At first she is deeply honored by what she takes as a measure of her father's respect for her professional talent. But immediately after flattering Ellen with his offer, George dashes her spirits by heaping her arms full of soiled shirts and tossing off instructions on how to launder them.

Discussion Questions:
1. Describe the insights this scene offers into this family's system of operation. What seem to be the typical roles and relationships of the father, daughter, and (non-pictured) mother? How do the family members handle changes in the system?
2. Discuss the climate and the messages in this scene in terms of the following pairs of concepts: content/relationship; confirming/disconfirming; verbal/nonverbal; equality/superiority.

Film: *Pretty Woman*
Year: 1990
Central Concept: Self-Concept
Approximate Scene Location: 60 minutes into the 119-minute film
Approximate Scene Length: 2 minutes
Opening Line: "The first guy I ever loved was a total nothing . . ."
Closing Line: "You ever notice that?"

Scene Description: In this scene, Vivian shares her story with Edward of how she became a call girl. Her history with men, previous jobs, and prostitution suggests that she has low self-esteem and has molded her self-concept from the negative appraisals of others. Even when Edward tells Vivian that she has potential, she says, "People put you down enough times, you start to believe it." The experiences of her life make it difficult for Vivian to see herself as worthwhile.

Discussion Questions:
1. How is Vivian's self-concept related to reflected appraisal?
2. Why is it that "the bad stuff is easier to believe" when forming a self-concept?
3. How might Vivian's occupation play a role in forming and perpetuating her self-concept?

Film: *P.S. I Love You*
Year: 2007
Central Concept: Conflict
Related Concepts: Gender, Punctuation, Content and Relational Messages, Metacommunication, Relational Dialectics
Approximate Scene Location: Opening scene
Approximate Scene Length: 6 minutes
Opening Line: Holly and Gerry are shown walking up steps leaving the subway.
Closing Line: "Kiss mine...in English!"

Scene Description: Holly and Gerry are two young people passionately in love with each other. In fact, quite often their passion boils over into a heated argument. This scene begins with Gerry knowing that Holly is angry with him, but not knowing exactly why – her nonverbal communication speaks for itself. As he questions her about the source of this conflict, additional issues about their relationship start to seep out. Gerry becomes frustrated with Holly's insistence that what he says and what he means are two different things, and Holly is equally irritated with Gerry's cavalier approach to their relationship. The scene works on several levels, and mostly because it taps into many students' notions about romantic conflict.

Discussion Questions:
1. What styles of conflict do Holly and Gerry express in this scene? How might their gender differences influence these styles?
2. Holly and Gerry seem to have different perceptions of punctuation, when this conflict really started and by whom. How is Holly punctuating their argument? Gerry?
3. Explain how the scene illustrates the content and relational dimensions of messages, and identify examples of metacommunication.
4. Which dialectical tension is Holly experiencing, concerning her job and having a baby? How is she choosing to manage this tension? What is Gerry's response?
5. What could Holly and Gerry do to manage this conflict, and future ones, more competently?

Film: *The Pursuit of Happyness*
Year: 2006
Central Concept: Self-Fulfilling Prophecy
Related Concepts: Self-Actualization, Emotional Intelligence
Approximate Scene Location: 107 minutes into the 117-minute movie
Approximate Scene Length: 4 minutes
Opening Line: "Chris, thank you very much."
Closing Line: "Christopher, come here."

Scene Description: Struggling salesman Chris Gardner pursues a life-changing professional endeavor of becoming a stockbroker under the tremendous pressures of homelessness, tax seizure, jail time, and single parenthood. While caring for his son without any outside help, Gardner endures a grueling unpaid internship. He is determined to win employment in a program where only one of the twenty interns receives a job offer. In this powerful scene, Gardner interacts with his mentor at the end of his internship, when a hiring decision is being made by the company.

Discussion Questions:
1. Describe how Gardner communicates competently with his client and colleagues.
2. Apply the term "self-fulfilling prophecy" to Gardner's life story.
3. How does the final scene exemplify a moment of self-actualization for Gardner?
4. Given the extreme pressures placed on him, explain Gardner's apparent emotional intelligence.

Film: *The Remains of the Day*
Year: 1993
Central Concept: Nonverbal Communication
Related Concepts: Relational Intimacy, Relational Dialectics, Emotions
Approximate Scene Location: 87 minutes into the 135-minute film
Approximate Scene Length: 3 minutes
Opening Line: "Flowers" (Miss Kenton) "Hmm?" "Flowers."
Closing Line: "I really must ask you please not to disturb the few moments I have to myself."

Scene Description: *The Remains of the Day* focuses on the 1930s working relationship between Stevens, a reserved head butler of a huge English mansion, and Miss Kenton, the mansion's outspoken housekeeper. Stevens has learned to repress his emotions, which becomes obvious when Kenton surprises him in his den as he is reading. She invades his personal time and space, especially as she inches nearer and nearer to him. Kenton and Stevens have developed romantic feelings for one another, but his inability to express his emotions makes this situation uncomfortable, even painful, for the two of them. Does Stevens want Kenton to leave him alone, as his words command, or does he wish her to spend this quiet moment with him, as his eyes suggest? The contradiction between Stevens' verbal and nonverbal communication points to the dialectical tension of intimacy/distance in their relationship.

Discussion Questions:
1. Discuss the nonverbal messages being exchanged in this scene, using terms from this course.
2. Discuss the mixed messages in this scene. How and when do the content messages contradict the relationship messages?
3. What dialectical tensions are in evidence between Stevens and Kenton?
4. How did you feel as you watched this scene? Identify three specific emotions.

Film: *Sex Drive*
Year: 2008
Central Concept: Identity Management
Related Concepts: Computer-Mediated Communication, Self-Disclosure, Saving Face

Scene 1
Approximate Scene Location: Opening scene
Approximate Scene Length: 1 minute, 40 seconds
Opening Line: "We open up against Michigan in 2 weeks."
Closing Line: "I gotta bounce."

Scene 2
Approximate Scene Location: 16 minutes into the 109-minute film
Approximate Scene Length: 2 minutes
Opening Line: "What are you doing in there man?"
Closing Line: "Harsh!"

Scene(s) Description: Fueled by adolescent-themed humor, *Sex Drive* is a film fitting of the teen-angst and road trip genres. Although the film will not appear on any critics' top ten list, two scenes illustrate the process of identity management well.

Scene 1 – Ian is shown typing away on his laptop having a mediated conversation with a woman – except Ian's online identity does not match his face-to-face persona. Utilizing principles of selective self-presentation, Ian has created his ideal self online: a football player, physically attractive, and a smooth talker. (Note that some audiences may find the language in this scene to be inappropriate.)

Scene 2 is a face-to-face conversation, so Ian doesn't have the luxury of editing his words or misrepresenting his physical image. The real Ian is average looking, has difficulty talking with women, and works at a donut shop where he wears a ridiculous uniform. Here Ian misreads the cues of his female platonic friend, Felicia, and her disclosure of a new crush. Wanting to believe that Felicia has fallen for him, Ian mistakenly moves in for a romantic kiss. Watching how both parties attempt to save face during this embarrassing moment is both humorous and painful.

Separately, each scene could be utilized to demonstrate different forms of identity management. Taken together, both scenes provide a descriptive contrast between mediated and face-to-face self-presentation.

Discussion Questions:
1. Describe how Ian manages his identity online. What strategies of selective self-presentation does he use? What strategies do you use to manage your online identity?
2. Thinking about the concepts perceived self and presenting self, which one is Ian's online self? His face-to-face self? Speculate why he has difficulty aligning the two selves.
3. In the second scene, what strategies do Ian and Felicia use to save face during their awkward conversation?
4. Reflect on and describe an awkward conversation you had that was similar to Ian's. How did you manage the conversation? Were you able to save face? What did you learn from the experience?

Film: *Shark Tale*
Year: 2004
Central Concept: Identity and Impression Management
Related Concepts: Deception, Conflict Resolution
Approximate Scene Location: 75 minutes into the 90-minute movie
Approximate Scene Length: 4 minutes
Opening Line: "I am not a real sharkslayer."
Closing Line: "Sykes and Oscar's Whale Wash is open."

Scene Description: When the son of the shark mob boss is found dead, a small fish with attitude named Oscar is coincidentally found at the scene. Oscar takes the opportunity to toughen up his identity, posing as the "sharkslayer." Oscar soon learns that his deception and fake identity have ill effects on his life and relationships. The other main character, Lenny, is a great white shark and brother to the mob boss's son. Lenny has a sensitive side and a secret about his identity—he's a vegetarian shark who pretends to eat fish, but in reality is nauseated when forced to do so. In this scene, Oscar and Lenny admit to their deception and apologize to their relatives and friends.

Discussion Questions:
1. What were Oscar's and Lenny's reasons for telling lies about their identities?
2. Give a real-world example of presenting a false identity, and explain the likely reasons for this misrepresentation.
3. Describe the gendered expectations of Oscar and Lenny and why they lied to meet them.
4. Is misrepresenting one's identity ever ethical? Explain your answer, giving examples.

Film: *Shrek the Third*
Year: 2007
Central Concept: Self-Disclosure
Related Concepts: Linguistic Convergence, Reciprocity, Relational Development

Scene 1
Approximate Scene Location: 41 minutes into the 93-minute film
Approximate Scene Length: 2 minutes
Opening Line: "How humiliating"
Closing Line: "Help! I've been kidnapped by a monster trying to relate to me!"

Scene 2
Approximate Scene Location: 47 minutes into the 93-minute film
Approximate Scene Length: 2 minutes
Opening Line: "Look…Artie…um…"
Closing Line: "Yeah, I got that."

Scene(s) Description: For those viewers who saw the original *Shrek*, you'll likely remember Shrek's insightful analysis comparing ogres to onions – a scene practically written for social penetration theory. In *Shrek the Third*, viewers witness the ogre put his theory into action. Up to this point in the film, Shrek has had a difficult time building a relationship with young King Author (Artie) and convincing him to be the next king of Far, Far Away. In the first scene, Shrek exhibits incompetent communication: he yells at Artie, threatens to hit him with a club, and unconvincingly attempts to speak like a teenager. In the next scene, Shrek chooses to self-disclose intimate details about his own childhood and upbringing. Shrek gains Artie's trust, and their relationship progresses to another stage. (Note: A quick fast-forward is all that is necessary between the two scenes.)

Discussion Questions:

1. Describe how Shrek attempts linguistic convergence with Artie in scene 1. Why is Shrek unsuccessful? Can you think of a personal example of linguistic convergence, either as the sender or the receiver? Was it successful?
2. Apply principles of self-disclosure and explain how Shrek is able to gain Artie's trust in scene 2.
3. At the end of scene 2, which stage of relational development do you think Shrek and Artie have reached?

Film: *Superbad*
Year: 2007
Central Concept: Communication Competence
Related Concepts: Empathy, Cognitive Complexity, Language
Approximate Scene Location: 11 minutes into the 114-minute film
Approximate Scene Length: 1 minute
Opening Line: "Ms. Hayworth, I joined this class because I thought I would be cooking with a partner."
Closing Line: "Jules"

Scene Description: Seth and his best friend Evan are high school seniors desperately searching for one final party before graduation. Most of the time Seth's heart is in the right place, even if his foot is occasionally stuck in his mouth. In this scene, Seth attempts to explain to his Home Economics teacher the injustice of not having a cooking partner. During his argument, his language is sprinkled with vulgarity, and he insults his teacher's course, profession, and gender. While Seth does employ a few reasonable strategies to gain her compliance (qualifying his language, apologizing, and initiating subtle touch), his communication incompetence speaks for itself. (Warning: this scene contains some coarse language.)

Discussion Questions:

1. In what ways does Seth exhibit communication incompetence?
2. Consider the three dimensions of empathy. Describe Seth's success rate for each dimension.
3. Would you evaluate Seth as having high cognitive complexity? Why or why not?
4. Seth frequently uses the phrase "no offense" during his talk with Ms. Hayworth. What type of language device is this? Evaluate its effectiveness in this scene compared to your own use of this phrase.

Film: *Thank You for Smoking*
Year: 2006
Central Concept: Persuasion
Related Concepts: Ethos/Pathos/Logos, Social Judgment Theory, Fallacies of Reasoning, Ethics
Approximate Scene Location: 45 minutes into the 92-minute film
Approximate Scene Length: 5 minutes
Opening Line: "Pearl, we got company."
Closing Line: "No, Lorne. Either you keep all the money, or you give it all away."

Scene Description: Based on the novel by Christopher Buckley, this film is a satirical look at both the tobacco industry and the congressional lobbying system. Nick Naylor is the Vice President and lead spokesperson for the Academy of Tobacco Studies, an oxymoronic institution if there ever were one. Nick's job – at which he is quite successful – is to persuade whoever is listening that smoking cigarettes is not unhealthy. The film illustrates a variety of fallacious and morally questionable persuasive strategies. In this scene, Nick has been dispatched by big tobacco to the home of the actor who portrayed the Marlboro Man in cigarette ads. Now he is dying of lung cancer, and Nick is there to bribe him to keep quiet. What ensues is a clever example of illogical reasoning and unethical persuasion.

Discussion Questions:
1. Provide examples of ethos, pathos, and logos appeals made by Nick in his conversation with the Marlboro Man.
2. Use social judgment theory to explain how Nick successfully persuades the Marlboro Man to take the bribe. Given his high ego-involvement, plot out the Marlboro Man's latitudes of acceptance, rejection, and non-commitment, and arrange Nick's arguments along that continuum.
3. Describe three fallacies of reasoning that Nick uses in his argument. Why did the Marlboro Man not see these fallacies? Which fallacies have you found to be used most often in real-world examples, based on your personal observations?
4. In Nick's own words, his job requires "a moral flexibility" that most people don't have; in other words it's unethical. Discuss additional, real-world examples of persuasion that you have found to be unethical.

Film: *The Visitor*
Year: 2007
Central Concept: Identity Management
Related Concepts: Self-Concept, Self-Disclosure, Johari Window
Approximate Scene Location: 81 minutes into the 104-minute film
Approximate Scene Length: 3 minutes
Opening Line: "You know…I think that show was really kind of scary."
Closing Line: "It's kind of exciting not to know."

Scene Description: In Director Thomas McCarthy's *The Visitor*, Walter Vale is an economics professor and widower who has lost his passion for teaching, and for living. Seemingly sleepwalking through life, Walter has an unexpected encounter with an illegal immigrant couple (Tarek and his girlfriend Zainab) who are wrongly living in his New York City apartment. Instead of throwing them out onto the street, Walter graciously allows them to stay. And despite their many differences, Walter and Tarek develop a close friendship. Desperation strikes, however, when Tarek is arrested and faces immediate deportation back to Syria. What follows is an agonizing and heart-wrenching battle fought by Walter to free his friend Tarek. In this scene Walter and Tarek's mother, Mouna, are having a night out – a Broadway show followed by dinner. In this intimate moment, Walter reveals parts of his identity that before he had kept secret from Mouna, and perhaps even from himself. Walter's self-disclosure leaves him vulnerable, and the audience wonders how Mouna will respond.

Discussion Questions:
1. How would you describe Walter's public self? What about his perceived self? As he puts it, why is Walter "pretending" to be someone he isn't? Explain why his, or any person's, multiple identities could be so dissimilar.
2. Consider your own public and private selves. Are they similar? Dissimilar? Why?
3. Walter's self-disclosure is risky and clearly leaves him vulnerable. Speculate what effect this disclosure will have on his relationship with Mouna.
4. Use the Johari Window model to illustrate Walter's self-disclosure to Mouna. Draw two boxes, one before the conversation with Mouna and one after, to explain the change in information known between the two characters. Be sure to label the four quadrants within each box as Open, Blind, Hidden, and Unknown.

Film: *Waking Life*
Year: 2001
Central Concept: Linear communication model
Related Concepts: Ogden and Richards' Triangle of Meaning, Sapir-Whorf Hypothesis, Language
Approximate Scene Location: 11 minutes into the 100-minute film
Approximate Scene Length: 3 minutes
Opening Line: "Creation seems to come out of imperfection."
Closing Line: "That feeling might be transient, but I think it's what we live for."

Scene Description: As he strives to discover if he is awake or asleep, or somewhere in between, Wiley Wiggins listens to discussions on the meaning of life, free will, politics, existentialism, and many others. In this clip, Wiley is listening to a woman ponder the origins, functions, and power of language. The scene is successful because it breathes life into a sometimes abstract discussion of textbook terms, and does so in a visual way that many students can appreciate. The entire film is a series of philosophical, dream-like conversations between the protagonist and the characters he meets; the film was shot in live-action with digital cameras, then animators overlaid their drawings on top of the live images, creating a surreal effect for the viewer. Incidentally, some of the film was shot on the campus of the University of Texas, Austin, and several of the characters are faculty at the university.

Discussion Questions:
1. How does this scene illustrate the linear communication model? How does it illustrate limitations of this model, compared to the transactional model?
2. Explain how the scene illustrates all three parts of the Triangle of Meaning model.
3. Do you agree that "words are dead, they're inert."? Why or why not? Give examples.
4. Thinking about the Sapir-Whorf Hypothesis and linguistic relativity, discuss situations when you have felt constrained by language and meanings.
5. When have you had moments of shared meaning, shared narratives, with someone else? In what ways we can increase our chances of achieving shared meaning with others?

SECTION III
FULL-LENGTH FEATURE FILMS

Each of the film entries in this section provides information in the following categories:

Film Data: Year, Director, Length, and Rating
Characters/Actors: Principal roles in the film
Communication Courses: Appropriate classes for using the film (listed alphabetically)
Communication Concepts: Communication concepts that can be illustrated through the film (listed alphabetically)
Pedagogical Perspective: Introduction and viewing notes for the film, indicating audience
Synopsis: Summary of the film's plot and themes
Discussion Questions: Questions (and answers) linking the film to communication concepts

The discussion questions are the heart of this section. The questions posed are not the only ones that can or should be asked, nor are the answers given for the first four films the only "right" way to respond to the questions. In fact, you may argue with some of the analyses and interpretations. That's fine—any good discussion about movies should engender disagreement. The questions and answers are provided simply to offer you direction and data for analyzing the movies.

This book is designed as an ancillary for communication textbooks that focus on primarily on interpersonal and group communication concepts. Whenever possible, terms from these texts are used in the film entries, particularly in the discussion questions and their responses. The responses suggest some, but certainly not all, of the ways the discussion questions can be answered with concepts from the textbooks. It is likely that other communication issues beyond the ones identified can be found in the films. Thus, the entries should be seen as comprehensive but not exhaustive. If and when they stimulate new ideas, please share those ideas through letters, e-mail, papers, and articles.

(500) DAYS OF SUMMER

Film Data
Year: 2009
Director: Marc Webb
Length: 95 Minutes
Rated: PG-13

Characters/Actors
Tom Hansen: Joseph Gordon-Levitt
Summer Finn: Zooey Deschanel

Communication Courses
Communication Theory
Interpersonal Communication
Introduction to Communication

Communication Concepts
Attachment Styles
Commitment
Nonverbal Miscommunication
Relational Development and Dialectics

Pedagogical Perspective

(500) Days of Summer is a likable romantic-comedy that received critical acclaim in its short box office run. Typical college-aged students should be able to identify with the main characters, and their struggles with "modern" relationships. The film would be most useful in an interpersonal communication course, since it illustrates well the stages of relational development, commitment, and attachment styles. Viewing the film among a mixed gender audience should also spark discussion about male and female perceptions, and expectations, of romantic relationships. The film is rated PG-13 for some language and sexual material.

Synopsis

Tom Hansen thought he had found "the one." Like her seasonal namesake, Summer Finn blew into Tom's life unexpectedly, and he was a changed man – though perhaps not for the better. *(500) Days of Summer* opens with Tom severely depressed, mourning his break-up with Summer. In non-linear fashion, the rest of the film portrays Tom's reflections on their relationship leading up to, and after, their break-up. Along the way, we are treated to moments of misunderstood signals, ruminations on romance, and a conflict of commitment.

Discussion Questions

1. **Identify Tom and Summer's stages of relational development, including their coming together and coming apart stages. How are differences in commitment demonstrated in these stages? How do the characters experience and manage the predictability versus novelty dialectic?**

Given the film's nonlinear presentation, it provides a unique way of viewing relationship stages. Arguably, relationships themselves are not linear, and they do not follow predictable stages of development and decline. On the other hand, the film presents a compelling case study that they are.

Coming Together Stages:
During Days 1-8, Tom and Summer go through the Initiating and Experimenting stages. They exchange small talk, learning about each other's interests and similarities, and thereby reducing uncertainty – typical moments in these stages. On Day 11 Tom's version of the relationship is moving rapidly, since he talks as if he and Summer are soul mates with multiple commonalities. Instead, Summer labels their relationship as "friends" on Day 27, seemingly removing any chances of reaching the Intensifying stage.

On Day 31 that perception shifts dramatically when Summer kisses Tom in the copy room at work. Day 34 marks the Intensifying stage for both parties. While role-playing at Ikea, Summer again labels their relationship as "not serious." And although Tom agrees, they do have sex later that night – students might view this as a friends-with-benefits relationship. Days 45-95 signify the Integrating stage: Summer and Tom spend much time together, learning about each other and developing their own relationship rituals. When Summer invites Tom to her place, importantly not until Day 109, Tom believes they have reached the Bonding stage. There, Summer reveals a depth of self-disclosure Tom had yet to see, and a strong sense of commitment is apparent.

Coming Apart Stages:
The first sign of relational discord, and Differentiating, occurs on Day 259. Tom gets into a bar fight defending Summer. Afterwards, they have another conflict about the status of their relationship: Summer continues to label them as friends, while Tom believes they are more. Examples of Circumscribing and Stagnating take place at Ikea on Day 282. Instead of participating in their role-playing routine, Summer is noticeably silent and distant. Day 290 marks the Terminating stage, presented cleverly at the beginning of the film, when Summer desires to "stop seeing each other." Up until Day 402 when Tom sees Summer again, he is noticeably depressed and angry. Talking with Summer on the train, encourages Tom to believe that they are coming together again. And indeed there are moments of Experimenting and Intensifying for Tom, but they are not mutual. On Day 476, Summer sees Tom at their favorite park. There she explains how she realized that she has a desire for commitment, but not with Tom.

Regarding the Predictability versus Novelty Dialectic, Tom consistently desires more predictability in their relationship. Tom wants routines that couples share, and he wants commitment. Tom chooses Moderation to manage this dialectic, continually compromising his need for predictability with Summer's desire for novelty. Summer, on the other hand, is comfortable with uncertainty and a lack of commitment. Summer uses Denial to manage this dialectic, ignoring certainty and predictability, up until the moment that she terminates their romantic relationship.

2. **Use attachment styles theory to label Tom and Summer's perspectives on love and relationships, and identify examples of their attachment styles. Are their different attachment styles necessarily incompatible? Explain.**

Attachment styles theory by John Bowlby presumes that individuals learn about relationships by interacting with others. More specifically, as children we develop attachment styles based on interactions with our primary caregivers (e.g., parents). Bowlby identified four possible attachment styles, each a different combination of positive or negative views of the self versus others.

The secure attachment style has a positive view of self and others, characterized by confident and affectionate behavior. Secures are comfortable loving and being loved by others. Individuals with a fearful attachment style have both a negative view of self and others, and they exhibit strong insecurities about forming relationships. The dismissive style is a combination of positive views of self and negative views of others. Dismissives are reluctant to commit to others and tend to view relationships as unnecessary. Lastly, the anxious/ambivalent attachment style has a negative view of self with positive views of others. This style is characterized by inconsistent behavior: at times anxious/ambivalents have strong desires for closeness, while other moments involve denying other's affections.

Out with their coworkers at a karaoke bar (0:18:40), both Tom and Summer explain their philosophy about relationships. Tom, the idealist, argues that true love does exist. For Tom, relationship commitment is a healthy and natural outgrowth of being human. Summer, on the other hand, believes that true love is a myth. Her philosophy is that relationships are messy, she has never been in love before, and she should enjoy herself being free and independent.

Tom, it seems, might be labeled as having a combination of secure and fearful attachment. Regarding his secure style, Tom clearly has a positive view of others as lovable. Tom believes in the concept of true love, and he desires commitment with someone else. On the other hand, Tom does exhibit acute depression and insecurities during break-ups with Summer, and thus might also demonstrate the fearful style (Bowlby argued that individuals gravitate toward one style throughout their lifetime, although recent research suggests that combinations of styles are possible).

For Summer, a dismissive attachment is her preferred style. Although likable, and lovable, Summer perceives relationships as unnecessary – and she is not afraid to express that view. Her style shifts, however, toward the end of the film when she marries someone else after her own "love at first sight" moment. An argument could be made that Summer also, at times, shows an anxious/ambivalent style. There are moments when she desires closeness, though the majority of the time Summer demonstrates a need for distance.

If your students are more interested in love styles and not attachment, then a discussion could easily revolve around that topic. We would likely label Tom as having an eros love style, while Summer is more of a ludic lover (both for reasons mentioned above).

3. **Locate moments when Tom has difficulty reading Summer's nonverbal cues. Does Tom have poor nonverbal decoding skills, or is Summer difficult to read? What are their content and relational level meanings?**

There are several humorous scenes that illustrate the ambiguity of nonverbal communication. In one scene (0:14:47) Tom explains to his friends why his potential relationship with Summer "is off." While riding the elevator to their floor, Tom casually asks about her weekend. Summer replies that it was "goood" (said in a drawn-out way), and Tom misreads her paralanguage to mean that she had sex all weekend.

Moments later, Tom explains that he tried to tell Summer that he is interested in her, but she did not pick up his (rather high-context) signals. For example, when Summer asks if Tom needs anything from the copy room, Tom replies slyly, "I think you know what I need." Meant with a blank stare, Tom hedges and follows up with "toner." Later, knowing that she likes the band The Smiths, Tom blares their music from his computer as Summer leaves the office – his ambiguous nonverbal style falls on deaf ears.

Much later in the film (beginning at 1:00:25), Tom and Summer have stopped seeing each other. By chance they find themselves on the same train to a mutual friend's wedding; Tom is still in mourning over their break-up while Summer appears to have moved on. Long moments of sustained eye contact, smiling, and close proximity while at the wedding, all signal to Tom that Summer is still interested in him romantically. And when Summer invites Tom to a party at her place, he truly believes they are "getting back together" – there is a clever scene comparing Tom's expectations with reality. His expectations come crashing down when Tom learns that she is engaged.

In sum, yes, Tom does have difficulty reading Summer's intentions through her nonverbal communication, and these examples point toward the ambiguous nature of nonverbal cues. Perhaps students might regard Summer's style, and Tom's inability to read her, as a gender difference – a discussion of that possibility could be worthwhile.

AMERICAN TEEN

Film Data
Year: 2008
Director: Nanette Burstein
Length: 95 Minutes
Rated: PG-13

Characters/Actors
Hannah Bailey: Herself
Colin Clemens: Himself
Megan Krizmanich: Herself
Mitch Reinholt: Himself
Jake Tusing: Himself

Communication Courses
Interpersonal Communication
Mass Media and Society

Communication Concepts
Computer-Mediated Communication
Family Systems
Public/Private Self and Identity Management
Self-Concept/Looking-Glass Self/Self-Fulfilling Prophecy
Stereotypes/Prototypes/Scripts

Pedagogical Perspective

American Teen is perhaps this generation's version of *The Breakfast Club*, complete with all the requisite high school stereotypes. Indeed, one version of the documentary's marketing poster has the characters dressed to resemble their *The Breakfast Club* counterparts; the director, Nanette Burstein, claims the connection was serendipitous. Regardless, students should have little difficulty relating to this film. Burstein focuses her lens squarely on the five main characters, documenting their triumphs and struggles during their senior year of high school in Warsaw, Indiana. Self-fulfilling prophecy, identity management, and computer-mediated communication are a few concepts the film illustrates. At times the scenes do feel scripted, yet this stylized documentary likely has greater student appeal than traditional versions of the genre. The film is rated PG-13 for some strong language, sexual material, some drinking and brief smoking – all by teens.

Synopsis

It is their senior year of high school in small Warsaw, Indiana. What happens this year will have a strong influence on the future lives of five students. In this documentary we learn about the ups and downs of Hannah, Colin, Megan, Mitch, and Jake. Like a reality television show, the cameras follow the characters everywhere and document their most intimate moments. Will Hannah break free from this small-town life? Will Colin get the basketball scholarship he desires? And will Jake finally find true love? Each of these questions is answered in *American Teen*.

1. **The five main characters (Hannah, Colin, Megan, Mitch, and Jake) are prototypical American high school students, each representing a certain clique. What stereotype does each character fulfill? What scripts do the characters follow? Choose two of the five main characters and analyze their self-concept. Use the terms "looking-glass self" and "self-fulfilling prophecy" in your analysis.**

Hannah Bailey – Hannah fills the rebel stereotype. She readily admits that she does not fit in with her conservative community, and she cannot wait to leave Warsaw. She loves to draw, paint, and make art – anything that channels her creative energies. Hannah follows the script of the outsider. She is not part of any club or extracurricular activity, and more importantly she does not want to be. When Hannah starts dating fellow character Mitch, she is suddenly thrown into the popular crowd, with unfortunate but not surprising consequences. In one of the film's animated sequences, Hannah reveals her looking-glass self: she does not like who she is. Granted, at least part of her self-esteem may be biologically related to her mother's depression. Not fitting in at school, feeling like she is teased by her peers, living with her grandmother after practically being abandoned by her parents – each of these events also relates to Hannah's negative self-concept.

Colin Clemens – Colin portrays the jock of the film. Because of his athletic prowess on the basketball court, Colin navigates the popular crowd. Apparently high school basketball is everything in Warsaw, and Colin is treated like a hero. True to his script, Colin shoulders the emotional burden of every win – and loss. He also has the additional challenge of following in the footsteps of his father, himself a legendary figure in Warsaw basketball history and a darn good Elvis impersonator. Although popular, funny, and easygoing among his friends, we can see Colin's struggle to step outside his father's shadow and find his own identity.

Megan Krizmanich – Megan is the queen bee of Warsaw High School. Equally admired and hated by her peers, she is perhaps the most complicated and misunderstood character of the film. Megan follows the script of ultimate over-achiever: she gets good grades, belongs to all the right clubs, volunteers for school activities, and still finds time to party with the other popular kids. Under that glossy veneer, however, is a troubled young woman. When Megan was younger her older sister committed suicide in their house. The loss of her sister left a hole in the family system Megan felt forced to fill. She constantly seeks approval from her father, even as he sets her up to disappoint him. She acts out her frustrations and constant high expectations by drinking, vandalizing, and simply being obnoxious to her so-called friends. It is tempting to dislike Megan and cast her aside. Given a chance, however, she becomes one of the more sympathetic characters of the film.

Mitch Reinholt – Mitch is typecast as the heartthrob. He is the least documented character of the film. Handsome and athletic, Mitch's script is a more subdued Colin. He also might be the best example of an inaccurate looking-glass self. Mitch knows that others see him as popular and outgoing, but that's not really him. Only when he dates Hannah does the audience receive a peek into his true identity – shy, somewhat goofy, and someone longing to just be himself. Predictably, Mitch succumbs to the expectations of his peers and breaks up with Hannah, displaying a role he is unable to discard.

Jake Tusing – Jake portrays the geek of the film, and he does not miss a beat. He fulfills all the qualities of his stereotype: he is in the band, loves to play video games, and has few friends. Socially awkward to the point of incompetence, Jake struggles forming relationships with others. Like his fellow character Hannah, he too follows the outsider script. Unlike Hannah, though, Jake longs for companionship with others. For Jake, having a girlfriend is his ultimate goal. Unfortunately for him, real relationships are not formed as easily, or heroically, as a character in one of his video games. Jake also represents the best example of self-fulfilling prophecy. During his animation scene, he reveals that an unfortunate incident in middle school gave him the geek label and made him "be so afraid" of who he is.

2. **One benefit of watching a documentary is that the viewer is allowed to hear what the characters really think, then to watch how those thoughts and feelings are translated into action. How do their characters' private selves compare to their public versions? How do the characters manage their identity in different contexts? Provide examples.**

Mitch provides a good starting point to examine public and private selves. Among his friends, Mitch is the handsome heartthrob. Quick with a smile or a joke, Mitch appears to glide easily through high school. When he dates Hannah, however, his private self becomes more pronounced. Alone with Hannah, Mitch displays his shy, almost nerdy self. In a voice-over he reveals his true feelings for her – he likes hanging out with Hannah. At a party among his peers, however, Mitch's public image and potential loss of face dating Hannah become more important and he suddenly stops seeing her.

Megan also represents a good example of the public/private self dichotomy. To everyone except her closest friends and family, Megan appears to have it all: attractiveness, wealth, and plenty of friends. Privately, though, Megan feels enormous pressure to live up to her family's expectations. For example, rather than lose face and disclose the source of her anger (the anniversary of her sister's suicide) to her best female friend, Megan becomes confrontational and doesn't speak to her friend for a week. In another scene, a decision by the Homecoming Council sparks Megan to channel her frustrations into vandalism. She also has a confusing relationship with her best male friend, Geoff. Publicly they are strictly platonic, impossible to be anything else. Privately, Megan is destructively jealous of anyone interested in Geoff. Megan's public self is wild, almost out of control. To the world, she is the most popular kid at school. Inside, Megan is lost, lonely, and full of self-doubt.

3. **Using computer-mediated communication to manage their relationships seems second-nature to these characters. Identify examples from the film when the characters used technology to manage their lives. Did the use of these technologies help or hinder their relationships? How realistic are the film's examples, from your personal experiences?**

Beyond dyadic face-to-face communication, the film also provides several examples of computer-mediated communication (CMC) and the use of technology. For instance, numerous scenes show at least one student checking messages or texting during class, and other characters texting while having face-to-face conversations. When Lorrin breaks up with Jake, she is more interested in her cell phone screen than making eye contact with him; the cause of their break-up, Lorrin cheating on Jake, also began through texting. And Jake himself would rather play video games and inhabit a virtual world instead of interacting with real people. All of these examples may seem commonplace and ordinary for this age group. Yet, the film shows the ubiquity of technology in young persons' lives, and the continual distractions that often accompany the technology.

One specific theory of CMC, social context cues, argues that technology causes its users to feel less inhibited during interaction. In other words, persons will say and do things via CMC that they would not do face-to-face. One example from the film involves Megan, her best male friend Geoff, and another girl (Erica) who is interested in Geoff. Erica emails Geoff a picture of herself, topless. Megan becomes jealous and in what appears to be a matter of minutes the picture is circulated electronically throughout the entire high school. In the aftermath, we see Erica tearfully explain what happened to her and how she feels. In a shorter, though still painful, example, Mitch breaks up with Hannah via a text message. His choice of medium to terminate the relationship says something about his commitment to Hannah, or at least his immaturity.

4. **The film also provides insight into the characters' relationships with their families. Choose Hannah, Megan, or Colin, and analyze their family system. How is power expressed by the parents and their children? What double-binds do the parents create? What roles do other members play in their family?**

Hannah – Hannah's family has its own set of issues because of her mother's depression and her father's absence. Living with her grandmother, we don't see many interactions between Hannah and her parents. Those few scenes do offer a peek into their family system. In one scene, Hannah's father is there to encourage her to go back to school, even driving her in personally. He performs the role of enabler, however, when he ultimately backs down and allows Hannah to continue to miss school. Hannah's mother, in contrast, demonstrates the one-up position. In another scene, she literally tells Hannah that "you are not special…we've always tried to teach you that." Now Hannah's self-concept makes sense.

Megan – Megan's family provides clear examples of family systems and homeostasis. Megan's older sister was the hero of her family. When she committed suicide that role went vacant, the family was out of balance, and Megan felt the logical force to fill that role. The interaction patterns between Megan and her father are also noteworthy. Megan experiences pressure from her father to attend Notre Dame, his alma mater, and he often places her in a double-bind. For example, in one scene her father tells her not to be "disappointed for me" if she is not accepted. Yet, because the message comes from her father, someone in a powerful position whom Megan admires, that statement is a no-win situation for her. If she is accepted, he will be proud of her because he is her father; if she is not accepted, he will not be disappointed – because he is her father. Clearly Megan can't win.

Colin – Colin's relationship with his father presents additional examples of interaction patterns and double-binds, though Colin's dad uses a different strategy. We witness several scenes making it obvious that Colin looks up to his dad, he has power over Colin. With that in mind, Colin's dad is more subtle exercising his power: he chooses to use humor. In front of Colin's friends, his dad teases him about his grades, the chances of getting a scholarship, and his basketball team. Colin's double-bind occurs before an important basketball game. His dad tells him that his performance tonight will likely determine a college scholarship. But he tells Colin not to worry, it's just another game. His dad also says that without a scholarship, his family cannot afford to send him to college – but again don't worry about it, it's just another game. Given these confusing messages, it's no surprise Colin struggles to play well in the game

.

BABEL

Film Data
Year: 2006
Director: Alejandro González Iñárritu
Length: 143 minutes
Rated: R

Characters/Actors
Richard: Brad Pitt
Susan: Cate Blanchett
Amelia: Adriana Barraza
Santiago: Gael García Bernal
Chieko: Rinko Kikuchi

Communication Courses
Intercultural Communication
Interpersonal Communication

Communication Concepts
Interpersonal and Impersonal Communication
Needs Met by Communication
Perception and Stereotyping

Pedagogical Perspective

This film may require some preparation to keep students' interest. The introductions to the different families, cultures, and locations are slow and seemingly unrelated. From the middle of the movie on, however, illustrations of communication concepts are plentiful.

Synopsis

In the remote Moroccan desert, tragedy strikes when an errant rifle shot seriously injures Susan (Blanchett), as she and her husband Richard (Pitt) confront the misery of their unhappy marriage. This accident starts a chain of events that connect the residents of a North African village, the American couple, their nanny Amelia (Barraza) and her son Santiago (García Bernal), and Chieko (Kikuchi), a rebellious deaf Japanese teenager. As the film's promotional materials proclaim, this complicated story "demonstrates the necessity and importance of human communication."

1. Provide examples of problematic communication in the film.

Examples of problematic communication are plentiful in this film. For example, after Susan is accidentally shot while on a bus tour, the international press mistakenly stereotypes the incident a "terrorist attack." When Amelia becomes lost in the desert after a botched border crossing from Mexico, immigration officials treat her as a criminal who doesn't care for the children she loves dearly. Chieko's feelings of isolation and pain lead her to treat her sincere father harshly and to fabricate stories about her mother. In each of these cases, outcomes would have been more positive if the communicators involved had possessed the care and skill to understand others and express themselves more effectively.

2. Explain how the film illustrates four types of needs met by communication.

All four needs of communication—physical, identity, social, and practical—are depicted in *Babel*. For example, on the physical level, Richard interacts with Moroccan villagers and unsympathetic fellow tourists to get medical care for his gravely injured wife. We see identity needs illustrated as nanny Amelia struggles to present herself to immigration authorities as a credible caregiver when she frantically seeks help in locating the lost children who have been in her care. The social dimension of communication is illustrated most poignantly in Chieko's desperate attempts to seek affirmation from friends and strangers. On the practical/instrumental level, we see the struggle of the Moroccan boys responsible for Susan's injury and their family to deal with the police who regard them as criminals.

3. Provide examples of impersonal and interpersonal relationships in the film. Discuss how some of these relationships change over the course of the movie.

Some relationships shift from impersonal to interpersonal as the stories unfold. American tourists Richard and Susan are emotionally distant at first, but as a result of her life-threatening injury are reunited emotionally. Chieko and her father argue over his lack of attention to her, and over misconceptions about her mother's death. By the film's end, however, they each let go of the need to be correct, and manage to see other relationships are heartbreakingly impersonal: immigration officers as they pursue Amelia in the desert; the fellow tourists who abandon Richard and Susan at the hour of their greatest need, and the Moroccan police who pursue the young shooter and his family.

BOYZ N THE HOOD

Film Data
Year: 1991
Director: John Singleton
Length: 112 minutes
Rated: R

Characters/Actors
Tre Styles: Cuba Gooding
Doughboy: Ice Cube
Ricky Baker: Morris Chestnut
Furious (Fury) Styles: Laurence Fishburne
Brandi: Nia Long
Mrs. Baker: Tyra Ferrell
Reva Styles: Angela Bassett

Communication Courses
Family Communication
Interpersonal Communication

Communication Concepts
Communication Climate
Conflict
Self-Concept

Pedagogical Perspective

This is a powerful movie that offers an important glimpse into a world that is rarely depicted in Hollywood films. The language is rough and the violence is graphic, but so are the streets of South Central Los Angeles. *Boyz* takes place in a black, urban, crime-ridden neighborhood, and involves a stark depiction of family life, illustrating the power of confirming/disconfirming communication.

In an advanced interpersonal communication course, I juxtapose *Boyz in the Hood* with the movie *Ordinary People.* The differences are striking: *Boyz* takes place in a black, urban, crime-ridden neighborhood; *People* takes place in a white, suburban, serene neighborhood. The similarities are also striking: Both stories involve pairs of brothers who are loved/unloved by their mothers; both movies show fathers investing (against all odds) in their sons; both movies illustrate the power of confirming/disconfirming communication. The moral is that despite their cultural differences, the families in these films face similar issues in their relationships and communication.

Synopsis

Boyz N the Hood offers a rare glimpse into the mean streets of (and friendships within) a South Central Los Angeles neighborhood. Tre (Gooding), Doughboy (Cube), and Ricky (Chestnut) become lifelong pals after Tre moves into the neighborhood to live with his father, Furious "Fury" Styles (Fishburne). Ricky and Doughboy, half brothers being raised by a single mother, choose different paths while growing up. Doughboy's life is filled with crime, gang life, and "hangin' out." Ricky is a star football player who pursues a college scholarship as a ticket out of "the hood." Tre is a model of strength and character, due in large part to his father's guidance. Fury disciplines, mentors, and befriends Tre; as a result, Tre has a solid personal and moral foundation.

Although the story is set on a pleasant-looking street, the threat of gangs, drugs, and violence is ever-present (particularly at night, when the streets become a war zone). At several points in the movie, Fury offers compelling arguments about the problems of (and solutions for) their neighborhood and their culture. Ricky, who listens to and respects Tre's dad, nevertheless becomes a victim of a gang shooting. Ricky's murder pushes Tre to the brink; he wants revenge for his best friend's death. Instead, he takes the high road and walks away. The movie's endnotes declare what would be easy to guess: Doughboy becomes another victim of "the hood," while Tre goes on to college.

Discussion Questions

1. **Discuss the differences in Tre's, Ricky's, and Doughboy's self-concepts. Explain how they are affected by reflected appraisal and confirming/disconfirming messages.**

Tre's strong self-concept is a reflection of his parents' positive appraisal—particularly his father's. Even when Fury disciplines Tre, he sends the message that he cares about and loves his son. "I'm trying to teach you how to be responsible," Fury explains, "unlike your little friends across the street. They don't have anybody to show them how to do that." In a warning that proves to be prophetic, he concludes, "You're gonna see how they end up, too."

In another scene, Fury takes Tre on a walk and asks him if he is a leader or a follower. When Tre says he is a leader, Fury asks him to recite the "three rules." Tre responds, "Always look a person in the eye. Do that, they respect you better. Two was to never be afraid to ask you [Fury] for anything . . . The last one, I think, was to never respect anyone that doesn't respect you back." Fury is pleased that his son has remembered his fatherly advice. As Fury notes later, and the movie bears out, "Any fool with a dick can make a baby, but only a real man can raise his children."

Ricky has a relatively strong self-concept, due in part to the many confirming messages he receives from his mother. "I always knew you would amount to something," Mrs. Baker tells Ricky. "You make your mama proud." Unfortunately, she doesn't provide Ricky with the same guidance that Tre receives from his father. Toward this end, Ricky looks to Furious and Tre for mentoring and they become significant in shaping his view of the world. Ricky receives some lessons directly from Fury, such as when Furious explains the problem of gentrification ("Furious is deep," Ricky exclaims at the end of Fury's impromptu sermon).

In contrast to Ricky and Tre, Doughboy is subjected to negative appraisals from a young age. Mrs. Baker tells him, "You ain't shit— you're just like your daddy. You don't do shit, and you ain't never gonna amount to shit." The prediction becomes a self-fulfilling prophecy for Doughboy. Even his friends notice that Ricky receives preferential treatment. After Mrs. Baker yells at Doughboy, they observe, "She ain't like that with Rick. It's because they've got different daddies."

When Ricky and Doughboy get into a fight, Mrs. Baker slaps Doughboy but doesn't say or do anything to Ricky. After Ricky gets shot and Doughboy brings his body back to the house, Mrs. Baker pushes Doughboy aside to get to Ricky, then turns and yells to Doughboy, "What did you do? You did this! You did this!" At the end of the movie, Doughboy laments to Tre: "I don't got no brother. Got no mother, neither. She loved that fool more than she loved me." Doughboy's self-concept is shaped by negative appraisals, comparisons with his brother, and pessimistic prophecies.

2. **Discuss the reasons for, and approaches to, conflict in "the hood."**

Wilmot's definition of conflict is "an expressed struggle between at least two interdependent parties who perceive incompatible goals, scarce rewards, and interference from the other party in achieving their goals." In the gang wars of "the hood," scarce rewards and interference from the other party are central to the never-ending conflicts. Money is tight; upper mobility is limited; turf is small. As a result, drugs and guns offer quick (and shortsighted) rewards of cash and power. Violence begets violence in an ever-escalating cycle of destruction. When a gang shooting takes place, the immediate response is to seek and gain revenge—which costs both Ricky and Doughboy their lives.

Fury's goal is to help the members of the black community see, understand, and appreciate their interdependence. As he explains to Ricky, "It's the '90s. We can't afford to be afraid of our own people anymore." Furious is upset when Tre tells him he should have blown off the head of a black man who attempted to rob their house. Fury says, "Don't say that. Just would have been contributing to killing another brother." An African-American policeman who investigates the crime agrees that the robber should have been shot, because it "would be one less nigger out on the streets we would have to worry about." Fury looks at the policeman with disdain; the policeman challenges him by asking "Is something wrong?" Fury responds, "Yeah. It's just too bad you don't know what it is . . . brother."

The concept of black brotherhood as a means to "increase the peace" is also the theme of an impromptu sermon that Fury offers to a group of listeners in a vacant lot. "What we need to do is keep everything in our neighborhood, everything black. Black owned with black money. . . . They [the white establishment] want us to kill ourselves. The best way you can destroy a people is if you take away their ability to reproduce themselves. Who is out here dying on the streets every night? You all. Young brothers like yourself." Furious wants his neighborhood and his culture to handle their conflicts more functionally through cooperation, de-escalation, and foresightedness. Tre heeds Fury's call: He walks away from a gang shooting even though he wants to avenge the murder of his best friend.

THE BREAKFAST CLUB

Film Data
Year: 1985
Director: John Hughes
Length: 92 minutes
Rated: R

Characters/Actors
Andrew Clark: Emilio Estevez
Richard Vernon: Paul Gleason
Brian Johnson: Anthony Michael Hall
John Bender: Judd Nelson
Claire Standish: Molly Ringwald
Allison Reynolds: Ally Sheedy

Communication Courses
Group Communication
Interpersonal Communication

Communication Concepts
Critical Thinking
Group Cohesiveness
Group Development
Perception
Power
Roles
Self-Disclosure
Status

Pedagogical Perspective

This movie is ideal for college audiences because of its accurate and insightful depiction of teen and young adult issues (despite the fact that this movie was made in the 1980s). Students usually have a strong, positive reaction to the film and enjoy analyzing it from a communication perspective. The movie is rated R for its explicit language and topics (and a pot smoking scene). As a result, it may be inappropriate for high school students and may need a disclaimer (or an alternative, such as the 1939 classic *Stagecoach*) in college classes.

The movie clearly subscribes to an "ideology of intimacy." The moral of the story appears to be that openness and honesty—even with complete strangers—will make a person happy, healthy, and wise. Something to think about as you watch the film is "Do you think the members of the Breakfast Club will remain friends?" While those who love happy endings may answer yes, many realistically acknowledge that peer pressure from the members' cliques will keep them from interacting on Monday. If this is true, then the five teenagers in the movie have handed intimate, personal, and private information to people who may be their social enemies (or at least competitors) at school. In a worst-case scenario, their self-disclosures could become inter-clique arsenal in the weeks that follow. The pros and cons of self-disclosure are an integral issue in *The Breakfast Club*.

Synopsis

   The Breakfast Club takes place at an Illinois high school, where five dissimilar students are sentenced to spend a Saturday detention session together. In attendance is a "princess" (Ringwald), an "athlete" (Estevez), a "brain" (Hall), a "criminal" (Nelson), and a "basket case" (Sheedy). These titles identify the roles the students play during the school week. Because of stereotypes and status levels associated with each role, the students want nothing to do with each other at the outset of the session. However, when confronted by the authoritarian detention teacher (Gleason) and by eight hours of time to kill, the students begin to interact. Through self-disclosure they learn that they are more similar than different. Each wrestles with self-acceptance; each longs for parental approval; each fights against peer pressure. They break through the role barriers and gain greater understanding and acceptance of each other and of themselves. They ultimately develop a group identity and dub themselves, "The Breakfast Club."

Discussion Questions

1. How do the characters deviate from their normal roles during the detention session?

   Coming into the detention session, each character is fixated in a stereotypical high school role. Claire is the "princess"--an upper-class, popular socialite who is in detention for ditching class to go shopping. In contrast, Bender is a lower-class (and abused) young man who is perceived to be a sociopathic "criminal." Because Bender constantly questions and defies authority, he is a detention professional. In contrast, Andrew and Brian rarely defy authority. Andrew is a disciplined and driven wrestler who wants to break free from the demands of the athlete role in order to think for himself. Brian is a straight-A student who struggles with expectations of high grades—and is devastated about his recent failures in shop class. Finally, Allison is a neglected introvert who longs for attention and, in attempt to receive it, acts like a deviant "basket case."

   As the group develops during the detention session, normal roles are abandoned and new roles are tried on for size. In contrast to his usual low-status position, Bender has high status during the session because of his detention expertise. He assumes a leadership role in which his defiant questions and actions are valued rather than disdained. Andrew and Claire also deviate from the normal behaviors of their high-status school behaviors. Andrew abandons his macho athlete role when he cries in front of the others and Claire confesses to the pressures of being a virgin. Brian, the conformist geek, asks courageous questions and ends up sounding more secure and functional than his new detention friends. Brian, Claire, and Andrew all break from their normal roles by smoking pot with Bender.

   Allison, the basket case, steps out of her silent, unsociable role when Andrew shows interest in her as they walk to the cafeteria to get milk for lunch. Although she uses lies and deviant behavior to get Claire to confess her virginity, Allison provides wise observations that are contrary to her perceived role. Allison also steps out of role by allowing Claire to give her a cosmetic makeover, after which Allison begins to court Andrew.

2. What is the status of each character prior to the detention session? How does this change during their detention session?

   At the beginning of the session, status is determined by the hierarchy of the school's social structure. During the school week, Andrew and Claire have high social status. They recognize their shared status level and sit by each other upon entering the detention session. The two break into conversation about their mutual high-status friends while the other detention attendees listen. Brian is probably next in the school status hierarchy because of his intelligence, but he is also a "geek." He is usually ignored by high-status students. In the school's caste system, Bender and Allison are the social bottom-feeders.

   Early in the movie, it becomes clear that a different social order is developing. Bender is the expert at

Saturday detentions and is on a first-name basis with the janitor and Mr. Vernon (the detention teacher who acts tough around Bender but also seems to fear him). Detention sessions are clearly Bender's turf, and his status on Saturdays is high. Brian seems to recognize this when he gives up his seat to John and waits for John to take off his coat before he removes his own. As is true of high-status members, John begins making and breaking norms. He is the first to break the principal's explicit rule of "no one moves from their seats." He also breaks the implicit rule of respect for authority when he tears up a library book and when he removes a screw out of the library door so it will not remain open.

The removal of the screw demonstrates Bender's knowledge about the school and detention, and he encourages the other students to follow his lead. He knows that the removal of the screw will prohibit Vernon from keeping watch over them. His expertise is verbalized when Andrew demands that Bender replace the screw and Bender replies, "No, I know what I am doing—I've been here before." When Vernon demands to know why the door is closed and won't stay open, the group covers for Bender—again, following his lead in the norm of disrespecting authority. Bender also has influence over the group's decision-making. At one point he decides that the group will leave the library and visit his locker. Brian asks, "Why are we going to Bender's locker?" No one can answer him. It is clear that Bender has high status and a great deal of power in this group.

3. What power resources and discussion roles are exhibited in the movie?

Bender holds expert power because of his experience with detention. He knows how to prevent Mr. Vernon from being able to see the group from his office, which allows the group greater freedom. He also knows how to maneuver through the barricaded hallways on Saturdays. Beyond expertise, Bender uses punishments as power resources. He verbally (and even physically) threatens members if they don't respond the way he wants them to. He plays a variety of task roles in their discussions, such as initiator–contributor, information seeker, information giver, and coordinator. As devil's advocate, Bender calls into question existing norms and beliefs of the group members and makes them rethink their own identities; however, these behaviors also cross into fighter-controller role descriptions.

Brian exhibits expert power when it comes time to write the required detention essay. The group gives him authority to write their papers for them because he is perceived as their most intelligent member. In discussions, Brian plays various maintenance roles and is a feeling expresser when he asks the important question, "Come Monday, are we all friends?"

Andrew exhibits maintenance roles such as supporter-encourager by welcoming self-disclosures when they are offered. This ties into his task roles as information seeker and opinion seeker; he insists that when someone discloses a problem, they must follow through in sharing it with the group. For example, after Allison dumps her purse on the couch in front of Andrew and Brian, Andrew challenges her to confide in them. Claiming that she was the one who "invited" them into her problems, he asks, "What is it? Is it bad? Real bad? Your parents?" Allison responds, "Yeah." He asks, "What do they do to you?" Allison replies, "They ignore me." She might not have offered this information without Andrew's prompting.

Mr. Vernon tries to wield legitimate and punishment power resources. Brian and Andrew are quick to acquiesce to Vernon at the outset because they have been taught to be respectful. Bender, however, snubs Vernon's power by questioning his legitimacy and by showing his ambivalence toward his punishments. When Vernon threatens Bender with future detentions, Bender indicates that he doesn't care and goads Vernon into a verbal power dual. The scene illustrates that power is given, not taken, and that it is negotiated between communicators.

4. Discuss the group's developmental stages.

The developmental stages of forming, storming, norming, and performing can be seen in the movie. The group is formed because each student has broken the school rules; they are together because they are all serving detention (except for Allison, who at day's end admits she is there because she had nothing better to do). During the storming stage, both types of social tension are exhibited. Primary tension can be seen in Claire's statement that she doesn't "belong here." Examples of secondary tension include Bender's antagonistic exchanges with Claire, the shouting matches between Bender and Andrew, and Allison's strange outburst during Claire's disclosure about her parents.

Mr. Vernon attempts to set explicit norms by stating that there is to be no talking, no moving, and no monkey business. However, this attempt to establish norms is unsuccessful because the norms are not accepted by the group. Implicit norms develop in the group, such as yelling, questioning, disrespect for authority, and, most notably, self-disclosure. Many of these norms are initiated by Bender, which points to his power, status, and leadership in the group.

Regarding performing, the group ultimately accomplishes its explicit task—writing a detention essay—by assigning it to Brian. The group also has a number of less-explicit goals that it achieves. The most obvious is that they successfully kill eight hours of detention with a minimum of boredom. They perform many of the functions of an encounter group, learning about themselves and each other through intimate self-disclosures. They also band together in a variety of rebellious acts, from roaming the halls to smoking pot. All of these acts suggest a level of "groupness" that develops in a few short hours.

5. What factors contribute to the group's cohesiveness?

The first factor leading to the group's cohesiveness is the amount of time and interaction they have with each other. While time alone does not insure the development of cohesiveness, the group has nothing else to do and plenty of opportunity to talk. After weathering some primary and secondary tension, the group starts to congeal when it identifies a mutual enemy: Mr. Vernon. An early indicator of group identity emerges in Bender's use of "we" as he asks, "Why don't we close that door? We can't have any party with Vernon checking us out." They begin to perform as a group after Bender removes the screw from the door leading to Vernon's office.

Cohesion is further developed through self-disclosure. Bender gets Claire to self-disclose about her feelings toward her parents. Andrew then turns and asks Bender to tell about his parents. This discussion is critical to the development of cohesion because the group members begin to see the similarity of their struggles and they identify with each other. Later, the group pressures Claire to confess her virginity. An embarrassed Claire calls Allison "bizarre" for lying to force the confession. Andrew replies, "We are all pretty bizarre. Some of us are better at hiding it, that's all." They all protect their self-concepts by putting on faces in line with the expectations that others have for them. Andrew describes his struggle to live up to his father's athletic expectations and Bender tells of his father's abuse. Thus, two very different characters find common ground, typified by Bender's comment to Andrew: "I think my dad and your dad ought to get together and go bowling."

As they band together to fight against mutual enemies—parents, peer pressure, authority figures, stereotypes, boredom—the Breakfast Club develops into a highly cohesive group.

6. Discuss the role that perception and stereotyping play in this movie.

In a quotation that begins and ends the movie, Brian reads from an essay that the Breakfast Club writes to Mr. Vernon: "You see us as you want to see us, in the simplest terms, in the most convenient definitions. You see us as a brain, an athlete, a basket case, a princess, and a criminal. Correct? That's the way we saw each other at seven o'clock this morning. We were brainwashed." These stereotypes color the perceptions of all the characters, as a variety of perception tendencies are illustrated (e.g., people cling to first impressions, are influenced by the obvious, favor negative impressions, and blame other's problems on their personal qualities).

While nothing appears to alter Vernon's negative perception of the students, the students learn to look past their stereotypes of each other. They empathize with each other's struggles, dismiss some of the inaccuracies of their first impressions, and discover that they are more similar than different. As they leave the detention session, their acceptance of each other is symbolized by Claire and Bender. They walk out of school arm in arm; she turns up her collar "punk style" while he dons one of her diamond earrings. Each student both takes from and gives to the members of the Breakfast Club.

THE BREAK-UP

Film Data
Year: 2006
Director: Peyton Reed
Length: 106 minutes
Rated: PG-13

Characters/Actors
Gary Grobowski: Vince Vaughn
Brooke Meyers: Jennifer Aniston
Addie: Joey Lauren Adams
Johnny O: Jon Favreau
Marilyn Dean: Judy Davis
Dennis Grobowski: Vincent D'Onofrio
Lupus Grobowski: Cole Hauser

Communication Courses
Communication Theory
Interpersonal Communication

Communication Concepts
Conflict Management Styles
Content- and Relational-Level Meanings
Language Styles (low- and high-context)
Listening Responses (supportive and non-supportive)
Relational Dialectics (independence-autonomy)
Relational Stages

Pedagogical Perspective

Because of the popularity of its primary characters, *The Break-Up* should garner immediate recognition and interest from students. Throughout the film students should easily identify with the frustrations often felt when communicating with their dating partners, along with typical advice they receive from friends and family members. And since the film takes an unusual approach within the romantic-comedy genre, students have a unique opportunity to analyze the coming apart stages of relationships. The film is rated PG-13 for sexual content, language, and some nudity.

Synopsis

The Break-Up is a unique romantic-comedy. Instead of the usual happily-ever-after plot, the film portrays what can happen when a couple struggles with the end of their relationship. Brooke is an art gallery assistant who wants more than anything else to have Gary want to work on their relationship. Gary is a tour bus guide who wants more than anything else to be left alone. The two are so incompetent in their attempts to repair their relationship it's no wonder they end in a break-up.

Discussion Questions

1. **Identify the relational stages and dialectical tensions Gary and Brooke experience, and describe how these lead to their break-up.**

The opening credits lead viewers to assume that after two years of being together Gary and Brooke have reached the bonding stage of relational development. The first sign of differentiating we see occurs early, in the film's "lemons" scene when a conflict erupts after dinner with the couple's family members. With different characters this conflict might have merely been a detour on the road back to a lifetime of happiness; yet, Gary's extreme desire for independence and Brooke's equally intense need for connection (a clear dialectical tension) in this scene foreshadow more trouble ahead. Indeed, this conflict disrupts their relationship so severely that they quickly move past the stages of circumscribing and stagnating, and begin to exhibit signs of avoiding: They start living separately, (yet under the same roof,) to limit their interactions. Later, they force their mutual friends to take sides. In another scene, Gary insists on sticking to their "Game Night" routine, only to have the evening end in another destructive conflict. Brooke invites Gary to a concert in a last desperate attempt to repair the relationship and move back into the coming together stages. Unfortunately, Brooke is so indirect that Gary fails to recognize her veiled strategy to get back together. When Gary finally realizes his past mistakes, he also makes an effort to repair their relationship. It is, however, too late and the couple find themselves at the final stage of coming apart: termination.

2. **Describe the supportive and non-supportive messages directed at Gary and Brooke by their friends and family members.**

As their relationship begins to unravel, both Brooke and Gary receive a host of listening responses from family and friends, with most of them being non-supportive and full of bad advice. When Gary tells his best friend Johnny O that he and Brooke are through, Johnny non-supportively makes a joke out of the situation by suggesting that he'll "take care of it." The first time Brooke explains her relational plight to her boss Marilyn Dean, she dismisses Brooke by instructing her to "take the day off, be sad, and get back to work tomorrow." Later, Marilynn encourages Brooke to make Gary jealous, with equally bad results. Not even Gary's own brothers can offer useful responses: Gary's younger brother Lupus invites him out for a night on the town so he can find a new relationship and move on, and his older brother Dennis pauses just long enough in mid-argument to provide Gary with pseudo-empathy and disconfirm his experience (e.g., "there's no room for feelings in business"). Only Brooke's sister, Addie, presents examples of effective supportive responses. She agrees with Brooke by telling her "you had a choice and you made the right one"; she praises Brooke for standing up for herself; and later she even gives Brooke constructive feedback when she encourages her to take responsibility for her own actions and recognize Gary's behavior as intolerable. Addie's responses are competent because they are both effective and appropriate for Brooke's situation. If Brooke had listened more closely to Addie and followed her supportive responses, she might have been able to successfully repair her relationship with Gary.

3. **Explain how both low- and high-context language styles are present in the film.**

At least one of the many reasons Brooke and Gary struggle to understand each other and find themselves at the end of their relationship, is because they utilize contrasting language styles of communication. Throughout the film Gary's style of talk is low-context—to a fault. At practically every opportunity he attaches literal meaning to what Brooke says. By contrast, Brooke's style of talk is much too high-context and ambiguous for Gary. From claiming that she doesn't like flowers when she actually does, to intentionally attempting to make Gary jealous when she really wants him back, Brooke expects Gary to pick up on subtle relational-level meanings without stating directly how she feels. Only at the end of the film does Gary realize that Brooke's style of communication contains both content- and relational-level meanings. Only then does Brooke express directly to Gary why she is hurt and what she wants from him. As Brooke tearfully, and finally, uses direct speech to outline how the relationship is no longer rewarding and actually costing her too much, Gary implores "I wish you would have told me, I'm not a mind-reader." Had they been able to at least meet somewhere in the middle, with Gary more in tune with Brooke's hidden messages and Brooke more direct in what she desires out of Gary to make their relationship work, perhaps they could have coordinated their meanings and avoided this downward spiral toward termination.

4. Identify the styles of conflict used by Brooke and Gary.

Most likely one other primary reason for the couple's relational discord is their choice of conflict style management. Rather than confronting each other directly and communicating their concerns more openly, as suggested by Brooke's sister Addie, the film is full of numerous examples of covert and passive-aggressive conflict styles. On many occasions the couple uses passive-aggressive strategies to one-up each other: The pool table, Brooke's use of her brother's singing group, her efforts at creating jealousy by dating other men, and Gary's strategy of befriending her potential suitors. When they do engage in overt conflict, their choice to use competition and verbal aggressiveness are equally ineffective at solving their problems. Similar to their uncoordinated language styles, both Brooke and Gary's failure to engage in competent conflict management helps to fuel their break-up.

BRIDGET JONES'S DIARY

Film Data
Year: 2001
Director: Sharon McGuire
Length: 98 minutes
Rated: R

Characters/Actors
Bridget Jones: Renee Zellweger
Mark Darcy: Colin Firth
Daniel Cleaver: Hugh Grant
Bridget's Mum: Gemma Jones
Bridget's Dad: Jim Broadbent

Communication Courses
Group Communication
Interpersonal Communication
Public Speaking

Communication Concepts
Communication Competence
Self-Concept

Pedagogical Perspective

This is a fun film that resonates with young women. Bridget's obsession with her weight, appearance, and clothing will ring true for many college-age females who are bombarded with interpersonal and media messages about thinness, beauty, and apparel. The movie also raises interesting questions about what Bridget wants in a relationship: Does she want a "good man" (Mark) or a "bad boy" (Daniel)? It appears she wants both—and the final lines of the movie suggest that Mark might be able to fill both roles. The movie is rated R for language (liberal use of the "f-word") and sexuality (including a brief nude scene).

Synopsis

Bridget Jones (Zellweger) is a single British woman in her early 30s who worries that she will die "fat and alone." By her own admission she drinks too much, smokes too much, and is overweight—all factors contributing to her fragile self-esteem. Her self-concept and communication competence (or lack thereof) are central features in her relationships with Mark Darcy (Firth) and Daniel Cleaver (Grant), both of whom vacillate between courting and dumping Bridget in a variety of romantic (and humorous) encounters. By the end of the film, Bridget decides which man truly loves her—and that she likes herself "just as she is."

Discussion Questions

1. **Describe how Bridget's self-concept is constructed (and deconstructed/reconstructed) through reflected appraisal and social comparison.**

Bridget overhears Mark referring to her as a "verbally incontinent spinster" who "smokes like a chimney, drinks like a fish, and dresses like her mother." His appraisal sends her reeling—and resolving, yet again, to change her behavior and appearance.

Daniel, Bridget's boss, sends mixed messages via e-mail about her apparel and physical attributes (he writes, "You appear to have forgotten your skirt" about her short and tight clothing, which is both a criticism and a come-on). She hears the message as a positive appraisal and wears even more provocative clothing the following day.

Daniel dumps Bridget for another woman who is younger and more confident—an appraisal he shares with Bridget, which devastates and infuriates her. This "other woman" also makes a disparaging comment about Bridget's weight, saying to Daniel (in front of Bridget), "I thought you said she was thin."

Married people cluck disapprovingly about Bridget being single and in her 30s with phrases such as "Time is running out—tick tock." Her mother tries to fix her up with various men but believes Bridget's apparel is part of the problem: "You'll never get a boyfriend if you look like you wandered out of Auschwitz."

Bridget is surrounded by media appraisals/comparisons: Pictures of thin models on her refrigerator; self-help books ("What Men Want") on her shelf; the movie "Fatal Attraction" (with the line, "I'm 36 years old; it may be my last chance to have a child") on her television; glamour magazines on her coffee table; and cry-in-your-beer music ("All By Myself") blaring from her stereo. These media messages scream that she has been weighed in the balance and found wanting.

Mark tells Bridget, "I like you very much, just as you are." This is music to her ears and wins her heart. She has spent much of her life trying to live up to social expectations of attractiveness, but Mark accepts her shortcomings and values her many positive (and non-physical) attributes.

2. **Describe Bridget's communication competence/incompetence in interpersonal, public speaking, and interviewing situations.**

Bridget self-discloses without much self-monitoring in her first meeting with Mark. This leads him to assess her as "verbally incontinent."

At a publishing company reception, Bridget fails miserably in a speech of introduction. She doesn't know how to turn on the mike, she is clearly unprepared, she unintentionally insults members of the audience, and she forgets a colleague's name. Mark later observes that she is "an appallingly bad public speaker."

Bridget doesn't fare much better when interviewing for a new job. When asked about El Nino (the weather pattern), she thinks the interviewer is talking about Latin music. When interviewing to work on a children's show, she makes it clear (with an expletive) that she has no children and doesn't want any. She tells another interviewer that she was let go from her previous position because she was "shagging the boss."

Bridget also exhibits moments of competence and self-restraint. For instance, she daydreams about introducing Mark to one of her colleagues by insulting both of them—but she restrains herself and exhibits more politeness than either of them.

DEAD POETS SOCIETY

Film Data
Year: 1989
Director: Peter Weir
Length: 128 Minutes
Rated: PG

Characters/Actors
John Keating: Robin Williams
Neil Perry: Robert Sean Leonard
Todd Anderson: Ethan Hawke
Knox Overstreet: Josh Charles
Charlie Dalton: Gale Hansen
Gerard Pitts: James Waterston
Mr. Perry: Kurtwood Smith

Communication Courses
Group Communication
Interpersonal Communication

Communication Concepts
Communication Climate
Conflict
Critical Thinking
Defiance
Group Development
Group Polarization
Self-Concept

Pedagogical Perspective

Dead Poets Society is set in an all-male prep school, but the concepts of conformity, authority, and defiance are universal in their appeal and application. This entry touches on only some of the communication topics illustrated in the film. Other issues that can be analyzed include persuasion, ethics, and critical thinking. On the surface, Keating is a "good guy" who gets the students to think for themselves and to stand up for their beliefs. On the other hand, it is worth questioning whether Keating gets the students to think for themselves or whether he merely gets them to think like him. Keating's radical ideas in the hands of impressionable teenagers lead to a variety of negative outcomes, most notably Neil's suicide. Is Keating responsible, at least in part, for Neil's death? Does he appropriately mentor the students he influences? Is it ethical to encourage boys to engage in behaviors that are contrary to the wishes of their parents and the school's administration?

Critical thinking questions such as these lead to spirited class discussions. (Warning: Most students don't like calling Keating into question—which is ironic inasmuch as Keating teaches his disciples to question authority).

Carpe Diem: Seize the day. This is the lesson John Keating (Williams), an unorthodox teacher at an all-male prep school in New England, wants to convey to his impressionable students. Keating is an

alumnus of the school, Welton Academy, and hopes to make his students as curious and iconoclastic as he was (and is). Keating encourages them to "suck the marrow out of life," pursue their dreams, and find their voice. He does so with unusual teaching methods, such as tearing pages from textbooks, kicking soccer balls while shouting poetry, and standing on desks to gain a different perspective. These approaches are frowned upon by the administrators at conservative Welton, whose creed is "Tradition, Honor, Discipline, and Excellence."

Many of the students are captivated by Keating's ideas and ideals. At his prompting, they form a secret club called the Dead Poets Society (DPS), whose primary activity is reading poetry in a cave in the middle of the night. Many of the DPS members experiment with "risky shift" behaviors, due in part to the effect of group polarization. Charlie Dalton (Hansen), an already extroverted student, assumes a new identity as "Nuwanda" and becomes the DPS's daredevil leader. Knox Overstreet (Charles), a quiet student, chases (and ultimately catches) a football player's girlfriend. Todd Anderson (Hawke), a shy boy who is in his brother's shadow at home, gains a sense of acceptance, confidence, and self-worth. Most notably, Neil Perry (Leonard) joins a local theater production and falls in love with acting. This leads to a confrontation with his authoritarian father (Smith). When the conflict seems irresolvable, Neil commits suicide. The school fires Keating, charging that he is responsible for Neil's death because he incited the boys to rebellion. As Keating leaves the school, the boys demonstrate their loyalty to him (and defiance of the administration) by standing on their desks and calling him "Captain."

Discussion Questions

1. Discuss the group development of the Dead Poets Society (DPS).

The boys form the DPS for various reasons, the first of which is attraction to the activities. Keating romantically describes the DPS as a rebellious and mysterious gathering for reading poetry, wooing women, and creating gods. Neil, a student suppressed and controlled by his father, finds the risk of breaking rules attractive, for he sees it as a way to establish his own identity and regain control over his life. Charlie joins for a similar sense of adventure. The other students are not so eager to engage in risky activities and are reluctant to join. Charlie and Neil persuade, pressure, and negotiate to get these students to take part in the DPS.

Norms are established at the first meeting (some are adopted from Keating's suggestions). They include the time (after lights-out at Welton) and location (a local cave) of the meetings, as well as the opening ritual of reading a Thoreau poem. Rebellious behavior (e.g., smoking, drinking) is encouraged and a ritual dance is developed. It is agreed that Todd will be the club's secretary because he does not like to read aloud.

Storming occurs when Charlie announces that he wrote a letter to the school newspaper requesting that girls be admitted to Welton—and signed it from the DPS. This causes dissension because he did not ask for the others' opinions on the matter and because it calls attention to the secret club. Charlie shows loyalty to his friends and assumes responsibility for his actions by taking the punishment for the letter. Similar acts of loyalty and support regarding Neil's acting, Knox's pursuit of a girlfriend, and Todd's assertiveness are the essential ingredients of the group's performing stage.

Neil's suicide puts the club to the test as the administration coerces members to blow the whistle on each other and on Mr. Keating. This leads to more storming within the DPS and causes marginal members such as Cameron (Kussman) to abandon their loyalty. Although all the members except Charlie sign the confession statement that is forced upon them, the core members of the DPS remain cohesive. They perform one final rebellious act together: Standing on their desks to acknowledge Keating as their captain.

2. What methods are used by Welton's administration to discourage defiance among the students?

The administration is proactive in encouraging conformity and extinguishing defiance. During the semester's opening ceremony, the students are asked to recite the "four pillars" of the school's philosophy: "Tradition, Honor, Discipline and Excellence." These ideals are ritualized with symbolic activities, such as lighting the candle of knowledge. School pride is further inculcated at the opening convocation with this report: "In her first year, Welton graduated five students. Last year we graduated 51 students and more than 75% of those went on to the Ivy League. This kind of accomplishment is the result of fervent dedication to the principles taught here. This is why we are the best preparatory school in the United States."

Once defiance is discovered in the school (in the form of a DPS letter to the school newspaper requesting that girls be admitted to Welton), the administration calls an assembly to extinguish the defiance and punish the deviant. The administrators begin with a call to reason: If the author of the letter steps forward, the other DPS members will not be punished. They then use seduction to remind the culprit of the reputation of Welton. Finally, after Charlie indicates his guilt by pulling a prank at the assembly, the administrators use coercion—paddling—to extinguish his deviant behavior.

After Neil's suicide, his parents demand an investigation. Welton's administration uses coercion to extinguish defiance through threats of rejection. The administrators pressure the students by calling them into a conference with their parents. During the conference, the students are threatened with expulsion if they do not sign a statement that implicates Keating. This process also pits the students against each other. Cameron gives in and tells the administration about the DPS. He then pressures the group to comply with the administration.

3. Discuss the communication climate and conflict styles in Neil's relationship with his father (Mr. Perry).

Mr. Perry's relationship with Neil is a struggle for control; all disagreements are seen as battles with win–lose outcomes. As a result, their relational climate is cold, particularly when Mr. Perry uses control, neutrality, and superiority rather than problem-orientation, empathy, and equality.

Early in the movie, Mr. Perry abruptly enters Neil's dorm room unannounced. Mr. Perry's control over Neil is evident, as Neil's transforms from a confident, relaxed young man into a fearful, squeaky-voiced boy, saying, "Father, I thought you had gone." Mr. Perry informs Neil, "I have just spoken to Mr. Noland. I think you're taking too many extra-curricular activities this semester and I have decided that you should drop the school annual." When Neil mildly voices his objection ("It wouldn't be fair"), Mr. Perry asks Neil's friends to excuse them, then drags Neil into the hall. He is oblivious to Neil's concerns but is very concerned about his own embarrassment: "Don't you ever dispute me in public, you understand?" He then takes control and asserts his superiority: "After you finish medical school and you are on your own, then you can do what you damn well please, but until then, you do as I tell you. Is that clear?" Neil capitulates and even apologizes for "taking on too much," although his demeanor and subsequent actions make it clear that he accommodates due to coercion rather than agreement. He chooses to lose the battle in hopes of winning the war at a later point.

After hearing Keating's teachings about "carpe diem," Neil decides to take more control over his life by pursuing his dream of acting—an activity forbidden by his father. He exclaims to Todd, "I found it …

What I want to do right now … I'm going to act. For the first time in my life I'm going to do it." Todd reminds Neil that his father won't approve and that he will need his father's permission to act in the play. Neil responds, "If I don't ask at least I won't be disobeying him." He forges a letter from his father, thus winning the conflict through covert aggression.

Mr. Perry finds out about Neil's acting through an acquaintance and comes to Welton for a confrontation. Neil knows immediately why his father is there and tries to turn the conflict into a discussion: "Before you say anything, please let me explain." Mr. Perry interrupts and erupts (with evaluative "you" language, control, and neutrality): "Don't you talk back to me. It's bad enough that you wasted your time on this absurd acting business, but you deliberately deceived me. How did you expect to get away with this? . . . You made a liar out of me, Neil. Tomorrow go to them and tell them you quit…I don't care if the world comes to an end tomorrow night, you're through with that play, is that clear?...I made a great many sacrifices to get you here, Neil, and you will not let me down."

Full of despair and hopelessness, Neil turns to Keating for advice. Neil says, "He's planning the rest of my life for me without ever asking what I want—I'm trapped." Mr. Keating advises Neil to assertively confront his father and to stand his ground. Neil takes Keating's advice and Mr. Perry reluctantly allows Neil to finish opening night. Neil's father comes to the play and is unmoved (and perhaps disgusted) by his son's fine performance (one of the lines Neil says while looking at his father at the back of the audience is, "If you pardon, we will mend"). Mr. Perry all but drags Neil out of the theater in front of his friends.

In the power of his own house, Mr. Perry speaks for Neil rather than with him: "You're going to Harvard and you're going to be a doctor—you'll have opportunities that I never had." Neil explains, "I've got to tell you what I feel." His father is neutral rather than empathic: "Tell me what you feel. Is it more of this acting business? If so, you can forget that." Neil hopelessly says "Nothing," knowing his father will not listen to his thoughts, feelings, and wants. Tired of lose/win episodes with his father, Neil engages in the ultimate lose/lose "solution": Suicide.

4. How does Todd Anderson's self-concept develop over the course of the movie?

Todd Anderson's poor self-concept at the outset of the story is due in part to social comparison with his brother, who was a Welton valedictorian. This is reinforced by an administrator at the opening assembly who remarks to Todd, "You have big shoes to fill." Todd also seems to get little attention from his parents, evidenced by the fact that he is alone on his birthday and that he has received the same, impersonal birthday gift (a desk set) two years in a row. His timidity is noticeable in Keating's poetry class, where he doesn't answer questions and is afraid to read aloud.

Todd's self worth begins to increase through affirming interactions with Neil. Neil encourages Todd to join the Dead Poets Society, but Todd is reluctant because he doesn't think he measures up. "I'm not like you," Todd says to Neil. "You say things and people listen. I'm not like that." Neil asks, "Don't you think you could be?" Todd responds, "No. I don't know." Neil convinces Todd to try the DPS, negotiating with the group to allow Todd to hold a non-reading position. The reflected appraisal of Neil, a high-status student, gives Todd a sense of value and importance. Neil includes Todd in group activities, praises his accomplishments, and shares personal secrets with him.

Keating also encourages Todd to come out of his shell, albeit in unorthodox ways. Keating makes a pronouncement about Todd in front of the class: "Mr. Anderson thinks everything inside of him is worthless and embarrassing. Isn't that true, Todd? Isn't that your worst fear? I think you're wrong. I think you have something inside of you that is worth a great deal." He then pressures Todd into facing his worst fear by having him stand in front of the class and create a poem. Todd spins out a beautiful poem describing his innermost fears. Keating and the class are deeply impressed. Keating exhorts Todd to treasure the victorious moment: "Don't forget this."

Todd doesn't forget it. At the end of the movie, when Keating enters the classroom to collect his personal effects, the room is thick with tension. Keating is being run out of the school in disgrace, yet the boys want to acknowledge their appreciation for him. Despite the protests of the administrator, Todd stands on his desk to salute Keating as he leaves, crying, "Oh captain, my captain." The other students follow suit. The low-status, insecure boy has turned into a leader.

THE DEVIL WEARS PRADA

Film Data
Year: 2006
Director: David Frankel
Length: 109 minutes
Rated: PG-13

Characters/Actors
Miranda Priestly: Meryl Streep
Andy Sachs: Anne Hathaway
Nigel: Stanley Tucci

Communication Courses
Business/Organizational Communication
Interpersonal Communication

Communication Concepts
Defensive Communication
Listening Behaviors
Organizational Culture
Self-Presentation

Pedagogical Perspective

The Oscar-nominated *The Devil Wears Prada* is a fun and enjoyable film. Almost anyone will easily relate to the character of Andy Sachs and be amused by Miranda Priestly's obviously poor interpersonal communication skills. Examples abound in this funny and dramatic 2006 film, making it simple to glean lessons for how to (and how not to) behave in the workplace.

Synopsis

Recent college graduate Andrea Sachs (Hathaway) becomes an assistant to the mercilessly demanding fashion magazine editor Miranda Priestly (Streep). In nearly every interaction between Priestly and Sachs, the self-absorbed boss demonstrates that she values herself more than others and cares little about communicating competently or positively. The workaholic diva harshly criticizes all of her underlings, ignores their contributions, speaks cruelly, dismisses them or leaves the room in mid-sentence. Priestly offers few positive cues (verbal and nonverbal) in exchanges with her colleagues.

Discussion Questions

1. **Which of Gibb's defense-provoking behaviors are utilized by Miranda Priestly?**

Miranda Priestly exhibits most of Gibb's defense-arousing behaviors, especially evaluation, control and superiority. Not only does she ridicule her staff's clothing and appearance (especially Andrea's); she also smugly dismisses their efforts with remarks like "The details of your incompetence do not interest me." Unquestionably, Priestly employs control behaviors seen when she dictates the smallest details about her professional and personal needs. Priestly demonstrates belief of her superiority in most of what she says and how she says it. In another scene, the fashion staff anxiously awaits her feedback about a clothing line. She signals her disapproval by not even uttering a single word, often snapping her fingers, dumping her fur coat and purse on her assistant's desk daily and constantly barking orders.

2. **Describe Miranda Priestly's listening behaviors.**

In nearly every exchange between Priestly and Sachs, the narcissistic boss listens selectively, pseudolistens to Andrea, or leaves the room while Andrea is speaking. Priestly offers none of the positive nonverbal cues that accompany active listening, such as nodding or eye contact.

3. **Describe some of the messages about body image and body distortion issues present in the film.**

The fashion model industry is notorious for weight obsession and this film shows that only waif-thin models, celebrated for rarely eating, are acceptable. In one scene, the message is made clear as Andrea asks one staffer, "So, none of the girls here eat anything?" He replies, "Not since two became the new four and zero became the new two." Andrea responds, "Well, I'm a six" and he states, "Which is the new fourteen." The viewer can conclude that a size six is big, eating is bad, and other messages that distort women's healthy body images. In many scenes, Andrea is criticized for eating anything from regular lunch food (soup) to carbohydrates. Another scene shows Priestly complaining about the quality of the runway models, remarking, "I asked for clean, athletic, smiling; she sent me dirty, tired and paunchy." To the typical viewer, these models look gorgeous and thin; however, the unhealthy message repeated continually is that thin isn't good enough and regular or healthy is fat.

4. **What disconfirming messages does Andrea send to her boyfriend and friends once her work at the magazine becomes her major focus?**

As Andrea sacrifices her personal life to the high fashion culture of *Runway* magazine and the demands of her boss, Andrea loses some of her simplicity and individuality, drastically changing her attitude, behaviors, and wardrobe. All of these changes affect her private life too, particularly her relationship with her boyfriend, her family and friends. She disconfirms them by not being truly present when they're together, instead answering her cell phone, text messaging or running off whenever Priestly calls her. Worse yet, Andrea arrives later and later to their dates and events, sometimes never showing up, even to important activities to those she loves. Her boyfriend and friends interpret these messages to mean that they are not valued as much as her new-found image and burgeoning career. Andrea learns that life is made of choices as she learns that she has sent messages about whom and what she values and views as her priorities worthy of her time and attention.

GRAN TORINO

Film Data
Year: 2008
Director: Clint Eastwood
Length: 116 Minutes
Rated: R

Characters/Actors
Walt Kowalski: Clint Eastwood
Thao: Bee Vang
Sue: Ahney Her
Father Janovich: Christopher Carley
Barber Martin: John Carroll Lynch
Mitch Kowalski: Brian Haley

Communication Courses
Communication Theory
Intercultural Communication

Communication Concepts
Adapting to Diversity
Linguistic Divergence/Convergence
Speech Codes Theory

Pedagogical Perspective

Buoyed by critical acclaim and strong box office receipts, *Gran Torino* is a film your students know and likely have seen. The film provides several examples of adapting to cultural diversity, along with illustrating speech codes and linguistic divergence/convergence. The film is rated R for language throughout, and for some violence.

Synopsis

Eastwood plays Walt Kowalski, a retired autoworker and Korean War veteran living out his remaining days at his home. In Walt's world, nothing is supposed to change: children should always respect their elders, a man should be able take care of his own home, and people should live with their own kind. Walt's worldview changes dramatically when he gets to know his Hmong neighbors, and becomes an unwilling mentor for Thao, a young Hmong man in need of direction. Despite his crusty exterior and callous demeanor, Walt becomes both hero and savior for the entire neighborhood.

Discussion Questions

1. **Analyze Walt's process of adapting to cultural diversity, including resistance, tolerance, and understanding. Identify differences between Walt's culture and the Hmong people.**

Unquestionably, Walt's initial stance toward diversity is resistance. As evidenced by his racist comments and adherence to stereotypes, Walt wants little to do with his Hmong neighbors. Instead, he shutters himself inside his home, avoiding all interaction with anyone who is not like him. When Walt "saves" Thao from the neighborhood gang, he does so purely for selfish reasons (i.e., they are on his lawn), not in the least to help his neighbors. When other Hmong people bring him food as a sign of their admiration, Walt throws it away and insists that they leave him alone. For Walt, resistance is a way of life.

Walt's resistance, however, begins to wane and move toward tolerance when he gets to know Sue. After rescuing Sue from another neighborhood altercation, Walt realizes that they have several similarities: they are both outspoken and independent people. And when Sue invites Walt to her home for a Hmong party, she teaches him about her culture. Walt learns that avoiding eye contact is a sign of respect, smiling masks emotions, and touching persons on their head is impolite. His tolerance grows when Walt samples Hmong food – afterwards he gladly accepts food offerings at his door.

Unfortunately, understanding comes in the form of violence. Walt realizes that the neighborhood gang will never leave Thao and Sue alone, and he vows to make a difference in their lives.

2. **Looking closely at Walt's communication style, how would you describe his language? What are the meanings and purposes Walt attaches to talk? Finally, contrast Walt's communication style with Thao's and Sue's.**

From the outset of the film it is painfully obvious that Walt disdains speaking with most people in general, and especially with others who do not share his worldview. Walt's style emphasizes linguistic divergence, not convergence. Instead of using talk to build relationships, Walt employs talk to determine if others are part of his group – more often they are not. From his pointed conversations with young Father Janovich to his forced interactions with his selfish family, Walt's linguistic style is at once direct, acerbic, and frequently belligerent.

On the surface Walt's style of language could be described as low context – he generally says what he means, and means what he says. Moreover, one purpose of talk for Walt is simply to convey information efficiently and succinctly. For example, Walt typically displays impatience when others are not quick enough to their point. When Thao mumbles something about jumper cables, or his family, or the neighborhood gang, Walt insists that Thao speak clearly and "get on with it." Walt believes talk is instrumental in sending information.

Looking deeper, we also realize another purpose of talk for Walt is to gauge one's mettle, to determine if someone can stand up for himself. Indeed, backing down from Walt in a conversation is a sign of disrespect and dishonor. If a person can take an insult from Walt and reply in kind, then he has Walt's respect. Walt's son, Mitch, never learned this lesson and instead perceives his father's verbal abuse as demoralizing.

In contrast to Walt's hyper-masculine style of talk is Thao's indirect, feminine style. Thao rarely tells others how he feels, instead allowing Sue and their mother to speak for him. For instance, when the neighborhood gang attempts to persuade Thao to join them, Sue speaks for Thao saying, "He doesn't want to talk to you…leave him alone." When Thao struggles to explain why he has to work for Walt to repay a cultural debt, again Sue and their mother speak for him. In Walt's world, Thao's communication style does not earn his respect – he is far too deferential for Walt's taste. Eventually Thao does adopt Walt's style, as evidenced in a scene when they are moving an old freezer from Walt's basement.

In Sue, however, Walt immediately finds his linguistic contemporary and she quickly earns his regard. Not afraid to speak her mind, Sue is straightforward with her talk. When Walt insults her, she insults him back. When three men on a neighborhood corner push her around, she pushes back. And when the neighborhood gang attempts to exert their power on Sue's family, she remains steadfast. Sue's independent communication style blends well with Walt's, and their similarity sparks both convergence and a friendship.

3. **Using speech codes theory, analyze Walt's personal and social identity. Identify examples when Walt teaches these speech codes to Thao.**

Speech codes theory is a framework to help understand a culture's meanings, rules, and conduct. In addition to a culture's distinctive style of language, speech codes theory also brings clarity to an individual's personal and social identity.

The dominant speech code that Walt operates from is "one's place in the neighborhood." At several points in the film, Walt bemoans the changes to his neighborhood: the Hmong who have moved in and taken over, how the houses have become worn down, and the general lack of pride that has befallen his community. Walt does not view his own increasing minority status as cause for losing his "place," however. On the contrary, Walt views, and talks to, his neighbors as if *they* are the outsiders: why did *they* move here, when are *they* going to leave, this neighborhood is decaying because of *them*. Walt also understands his place in others' community as well. When he rescues Sue from three aggressive men on a street corner, Walt admonishes Sue's date, "They don't want to be your friend…go back where you came from." In another scene, Father Janovich attempts to counsel Walt at the neighborhood bar. Walt insists that Father Janovich have a drink first, after all that's what men do in bars. Without question, Walt's social identity is defined by his place in the neighborhood.

Some of the more illustrative, and humorous, scenes about Walt's personal identity occur when he struggles to teach Thao "how to talk like a guy" – the speech codes of manliness. Walt takes Thao to the neighborhood barbershop, owned and operated by Martin. Peppered with profanity and laced with mock insults, Walt's conversation with Martin is code for how real guys talk to each other. When Thao practices this talk on Martin, however, he fails the rule of context: don't insult a man in his own business, unless you are already friends. Instead, appropriate topics of talk are complaints about work, your car, or your girlfriend – all manly things to say to other guys whom you do not know well. Walt then takes Thao to a construction site, hoping to pull some strings and secure a job for Thao. When Thao speaks with the site supervisor, surprisingly he gets the code right: Thao complains about work done on his car, looks the supervisor in the eye, and gives him a firm handshake. In other words, Thao's behavior symbolizes respect, honor, and proper place in the community – Walt's speech code for manliness.

THE GREAT DEBATERS

Film Data
Year: 2007
Director: Denzel Washington
Length: 126 Minutes
Rated: PG-13

Characters/Actors
Melvin B. Tolson: Denzel Washington
Henry Lowe: Nate Parker
Samantha Booke: Jurnee Smollett
James Farmer, Jr.: Denzel Whitaker
Dr. James Farmer, Sr.: Forest Whitaker
Hamilton Burgess: Jermaine Williams
Sheriff Dozier: John Heard

Communication Courses
Argumentation and Debate
Introduction to Communication
Public Speaking
Small Group Communication

Communication Concepts
Leadership
Persuasive Appeals (Ethos, Pathos, Logos)
Power in Groups
Small Group Cohesiveness
Social Judgment Theory

Pedagogical Perspective

As the title suggests, *The Great Debaters* is a film rich in moments of persuasion, both ethical and otherwise. Set within the backdrop of Southern racism in the 1930s, the film provides examples of persuasive appeals, latitudes of persuasion, and fallacies of reasoning. The film is equally effective at illustrating concepts of small group communication. Numerous examples of power influences are present, along with leadership styles and group cohesiveness. While viewers may become distracted with the romantic relationships that develop, teachers should push students to critically evaluate the arguments presented by the central characters. The film is rated PG-13 for some violent and disturbing images, and for language and brief sexuality.

Synopsis

The Great Debaters is a moving, inspirational story about how the power of speech can overcome prejudice. The film is set in southern Texas in the 1930s, a time and place of racial intolerance, where Jim Crow laws were still on the books and lynchings were a common spectacle. At small, historically-Black Wiley College, students on the debate team not only challenge each other, they confront the prevailing social ideologies head-on. With the help of their charismatic and eloquent coach, real-life poet Melvin B. Tolson, the Wiley College Debate Team gains national recognition as one of the first Black colleges to debate White students. Their prominence culminates with a nationally broadcast debate with Harvard

University. In the end the debaters gain more than a simple victory, they gain respect for themselves and their race.

Discussion Questions

4. **Identify examples of social judgment theory, including latitudes of acceptance, rejection, and noncommitment. How does ego-involvement influence the persuasive process?**

On a macro level, one could argue that the entire film is an example of social judgment theory. On several occasions, Professor Tolson expresses his philosophy of changing social injustice "one step at a time." In other words like the theory predicts, persuasion is a gradual and incremental process. This is a reality the debate team does not accept readily, especially Henry, for they believe they can change history all at once. Tolson convinces his students that change takes not only passion, it takes patience.

A more specific example occurs with the debate between Wiley College and Oklahoma City University. The debate takes place off-campus, already suggesting that a hostile audience full of biased-elaboration will be present. The topic is "Negroes should be admitted to state universities." This is a topic the debaters care about deeply (i.e., high ego-involvement), and so does the audience. For some members of the audience the message falls within their latitude of rejection. They have already made up their minds, and they quickly get up and leave. In her impassioned closing argument, Samantha pushes the boundaries of acceptance by calling for change today, not gradually, but completely. It should also be noted, having students analyze the counterarguments of the Oklahoma City University Debaters could prove fruitful to illustrate the complexity of the persuasive process. For example, one of the debaters commits a *post hoc* fallacy when he mistakenly claims that going to a state university will make Negroes unhappy, and an unhappy Negro couldn't possibly be successful academically. This may or may not be true; one's unhappiness could just as easily be channeled into motivation.

Likely the best example of the theory happens between Dr. Farmer and Sheriff Dozier. Already the audience knows that Dozier is a violent racist. Still, he's also aware of the power of the press. When Dr. Farmer comes to Dozier requesting Tolson's release from jail, he places a convincing argument right on the edge of Dozier's latitude of acceptance. Farmer states, "A mass slaughter, of Whites and Negro citizens, by Texas Rangers…is that really what you want as Sheriff of this county? If you let Tolson go home…I believe these folks outside will go home as well."

5. **How do the debaters utilize appeals to ethos, pathos, and logos in their arguments? Which type of appeal do you find most persuasive? Why?**

A critical examination of all of the debates should reveal the following: most of the appeals presented by the Wiley College team rely on pathos, while the majority of arguments presented by their opponents consist of logical appeals. For example, during their first debate on the topic of welfare the Wiley College debaters sprinkle their arguments with examples of "life or death," and their closing point relies on the evidence of "the look in a mother's face when she cannot feed her children." Their opponents, on the other hand, fill their propositions with facts on the rates and costs of unemployment.

In the end, emotions win. In the climatic debate with Harvard University, the opposition's primary argument again relies on logic as well. Even then, the audience's loudest response seems left for one Harvard debater's emotional example of his policeman father holding his dying partner in his arms. During his rebuttal, Farmer, Jr. seems at a loss for words. Relying on pathos, he vividly describes the lynch mob scene witnessed by the Wiley College debate team, arguing that "an unjust law is no law at all." Once again, passion trumps logic. Perhaps these examples say more about how to write a successful screenplay than it does an effective public speech, yet it is still worth examining.

6. Explain the factors or reasons why the Wiley College Debaters become a cohesive group.

There are several reasons why the debate team becomes a tight-knit group. First, two members of the team are attracted to a third. However, their attraction both helps and harms the group cohesiveness. Secondly, the team not only has the shared goal of winning their debates, they want to change the social fabric of the day. This motivation also creates a perceived threat from outside the group; what could be more threatening than losing their lives in a lynching? Sharing that experience of escaping the lynch mob together also increases cohesiveness of the team. Their cohesion is threatened, however, when competition for Samantha's affection increases, and when Henry breaks her heart. Still, the most significant threat to the group is the loss of their leader, Professor Tolson, before they are set to debate Harvard. Not surprisingly, this vacuum creates conflict among the members, as each vies for control of the group when they are preparing their arguments. Henry seizes the role of leader and delegates debate responsibilities to Farmer.

7. Identify examples of power used by the characters. Which types of power are effective? Which types are appropriate?

As a leader both in the classroom and with his debate team, Professor Tolson uses several types of power to influence others. First, Tolson possesses legitimate power because of his position. In addition, he demonstrates both information and expert power by his ability to quote poetry and scholarship. Whether he has referent power is, perhaps, arguable. His students do seem to admire him, and he does gain their respect during the film. Still, he frequently intimidates students and allows them to lose face when their answers are incorrect, a sign of coercive power. In one scene when Henry questions why Tolson writes all of the arguments for the team, Tolson ends the discussion by yelling "because that's the way it's always been!" On the other hand, when students do answer correctly Tolson rewards them with his praise. Perhaps Tolson is an effective leader because he utilizes a variety of power-influencing strategies, with varying degrees of appropriateness.

Sheriff Dozier represents the best example of coercive power. His intimidation is both verbal and physical. When he interviews two sharecroppers about their knowledge of the union, he not-so-subtlety suggests the negative consequences of their participation. Later, he physically beats one of the same sharecroppers, forcing him to reveal Tolson's identity. However, when a large gathering of people demand Tolson's release from prison, Dozier realizes his coercion only extends so far.

Lastly, Dr. Farmer provides viewers with the contextual nature of power. In the classroom and in his church, Farmer, Sr. is a giant of a man. He can speak seven languages, he quotes scripture with ease, and he supposedly was one of the first "Negroes to earn a PhD." Sadly, all of his power is lost when he accidently kills a pig owned by a White person. Instead of receiving respect, or even tolerance, Farmer is threatened verbally and physically. This scene illustrates well how power depends on the perception of others.

I'VE LOVED YOU SO LONG

Film Data
Year: 2008
Director: Philippe Claudel
Length: 117 Minutes
Rated: PG-13

Characters/Actors
Juliette: Kristin Scott Thomas
Lea: Elsa Zylberstein
Luc: Serge Hazanavicius
Michel: Laurent Grevill
Capitaine Faure: Frederic Pierrot
Papy Paul: Jean-Claude Arnaud

Communication Courses
Communication Theory
Family Communication
Interpersonal Communication

Communication Concepts
Privacy Management
Self-Disclosure
Uncertainty Reduction

Pedagogical Perspective

I've Loved You So Long is likely a film your students have not seen. In many ways their ignorance can be an asset because of the film's perceived freshness. On the other hand, a foreign-language film can be a hard sell for some students. Even so, we encourage you to make the effort. Lead actress Kristin Scott Thomas (*Life as a House, The Horse Whisperer,* and *The English Patient*) provides star appeal. Taken as a whole, the film is a dramatic illustration of one person's struggle to manage privacy under the most difficult situations. The film is rated PG-13 for thematic issues and smoking.

Synopsis

Juliette (Scott Thomas) is a lost soul, an empty shell of the person she used to be. Released from prison after serving 15 years for an unspeakable crime, she reluctantly agrees to be taken in by her younger sister's family. Her sister, Lea, desperately wants Juliette back in her life; Lea's husband, Luc, is less accommodating. One might assume that being free again would be a liberating moment, but not for Juliette. She struggles to merge back into society and to keep hidden the secret surrounding her crime. With the persistence of her sister and the empathy of others (Michel and Capitaine Faure), Juliette eventually lets down her guard. Through the process of self-disclosure she reveals her secret and starts to rebuild her relationships with others.

Discussion Questions

1. **Apply principles of social penetration to Juliette's relationship with other characters. How do depth, breadth, and reciprocity explain her disclosures? How do conversations and interactions with other characters reduce uncertainty?**

Social Penetration Theory (SPT) advances three principles: 1) self-disclosure is a gradual, linear process; 2) self-disclosure involves depth, breadth, and reciprocity; and 3) self-disclosure is regulated by calculating rewards versus costs. The film illustrates all three of these principles.

Even though Juliette and Lea are sisters, the opening scene of the film depicts the characters as virtual strangers. Having been separated for 15 years, their relationship has reverted to an early stage of development. In the car ride to Lea's home, for example, depth of self-disclosure is at minimal and the topics are trivial and light – typical of beginning relationships. At home, Juliette exchanges very little information with the other members of the household. In fact, one of the children comments, "Auntie hardly says a word." Luc obviously does not trust Juliette and considers her a burden (i.e., a cost); the children are inquisitive though Juliette does not reciprocate; and Papy Paul (Luc's father) is physically unable to speak. Not long after Juliette arrives, Luc asks his wife if Juliette has "told her why" – a reference to the reason she committed her crime. Taking a page from SPT, Lea responds with frustration that "these things take time…you don't simply come right out and ask her." Perhaps illustrating gender differences in self-disclosure, Luc cannot understand Lea's reasons for building up to the question. For him, reducing uncertainty with a direct question seems only logical.

As the story unfolds, so does the self-disclosure process. Gradually, layer upon layer is slowly peeled away as Juliette builds her relationship with Lea, and with the other characters. With hope that Juliette will reciprocate, Lea tells Juliette about her work, her relationship with Luc, and how they adopted their children. The sisters also share several activities together (e.g., going to cafes, swimming, playing the piano), which help to reduce uncertainty and progress the development process. Not until the final scene of the film, however, is Juliette able to completely reveal the secret surrounding her crime – even then she does so reluctantly. As predicted by SPT, depth of penetration takes time, and the film does a remarkable job of illustrating this slow process.

Additional scenes also illustrate principles of SPT. For instance, in Juliette's relationship with her parole officer, Capitaine Faure discloses relatively intimate details about his life rather quickly. Seemingly taken aback by his candor, Juliette does not reciprocate. Capitaine Faure reveals his motivation to confide in Juliette when he remarks, "Man isn't made to be alone." During subsequent conversations, however, they discover a common topic – they are both divorced. Now less uncertain and more at ease, Juliette evaluates their relationship as more rewarding and exposes more details about her life. Similarly, her relationship with Michel began in a one-sided fashion: Michel flirts with her and Juliette barely responds. Unlike the Capitaine, however, Michel is more restrained and learns to respect Juliette's boundaries; see question below for a more detailed description.

2. **How does Juliette struggle to reveal, or conceal, her privacy to others? What rules influence how she manages her privacy boundaries? What are the consequences of telling others about her past, versus concealing it?**

Petronio's Communication Privacy Management (CPM) Theory regards self-disclosure as a more complex process than does Social Penetration Theory (SPT). More so than SPT, CPM acknowledges the risks associated with disclosures, and how rules concerning the topic, context, and recipient are co-created in the decision to disclose personal information.

Unlike SPT, CPM recognizes that the desire to disclose personal information is offset by a conflicting need to conceal and keep information private – a dialectical approach. A wonderfully illustrative example of this dialectic occurs at Juliette's workplace. When she is hired at the hospital, her immediate supervisor expressly forbids her from revealing too much information about her past: she cannot tell others about her crime or that she used to be a doctor. After a few weeks on the job, however, the hospital director reprimands her for "being cold and distant" with her colleagues. He emphasizes that the employees are a team and that she needs to "be more open." Apparently Juliette has to follow the rules of workplace collegiality, and at the same time keep private the details of her past – not an easy task.

Unquestionably, Juliette has established boundaries regarding her privacy. She is extremely reluctant to reveal any details surrounding her crime, to family and strangers alike. Even when she was on trial, Juliette chose to conceal the reasons for her crime. While in prison, the audience learns that Juliette was labeled "the silent one" by guards and fellow inmates, again demonstrating her desire for seclusion. As CPM predicts, these scenes illustrate well how we feel ownership of our disclosures and hold onto them rather tightly. Likely because Papy Paul is locked away in his own physical prison and unable to speak, Juliette feels a certain kinship with him; he also proves to be a competent listener. Papy Paul's room becomes a sanctuary of sorts for her, a physical boundary, where she can escape the constant pressure and tension of maintaining her privacy from other household members. Indeed, Juliette's boundaries are anything but permeable.

While some characters respect her boundaries, others do not. For example, early in Juliette's relationship with Michel, he probes too deeply about her past. When she refuses to say more, Michel respects Juliette's boundaries when he replies, "Oh, it is complicated. I shall ask no more questions." Michel's mindfulness likely stems from his own mysterious past. According to Lea, he has his own boundaries regarding his family history. Unlike Michel, Juliette's social worker assigned to her case exhibits mindless communication. When the social worker remarks how stunned she was at Juliette's silence while on trial, Juliette firmly establishes that this topic is off limits by stating, "And you expect me to just open up…to you…right now?!"

Eventually her relationship with Michel progresses to a stage where Juliette feels less inhibited confiding in him. Likely, the turning point occurred at an awkward moment among dinner guests. When Juliette is cajoled by her fellow diners to reveal her past, the audience witnesses the angst felt by Lea and Luc. What would their friends think if they knew the truth? To everyone's surprise Juliette does just that: she says she was in prison. Because this is absurd and could not possibly be true, everyone except Michel believes she is joking. Such an unexpected disclosure must be false. Later, Michel reveals that he also spent time in prison, teaching inmates. Sharing this intimate detail and commonality brings Juliette closer to Michel, and the boundary around her past starts to dissolve.

KNOCKED UP

Film Data
Year: 2007
Director: Judd Apatow
Length: 133 Minutes
Rated: R

Characters/Actors
Ben Stone: Seth Rogen
Alison Scott: Katherine Heigl
Pete: Paul Rudd
Debbie: Leslie Mann

Communication Courses
Communication Theory
Interpersonal Communication

Communication Concepts
Gendered Language
Relational Dialectics Theory
Relationship Stages and Commitment
Uncertainty Reduction Theory

Pedagogical Perspective

Knocked Up is a film that contemporary students regard as a classic, and many critics agree. Rather than adhering to the typical romantic-comedy, the plot forces the primary characters (Ben and Alison) into a committed relationship before they are ready. The film also juxtaposes Ben and Alison's relationship with Debbie and Pete, a couple married 10 years with two children. Students in interpersonal communication and communication theory will have little trouble finding examples of relational stages and dialectics. *Knocked Up* is rated R for profanity, brief nudity, and references to drug usage. Instructors should decide whether the film is suitable for classroom screening or should be assigned outside of class.

Synopsis

Ben Stone is the quintessential slacker: he doesn't have a real job and spends most of his time smoking pot with his like-minded friends. Alison Scott, on the other hand, is the anti-Ben. Smart, attractive, and successful in her work, Alison seems to have the world at her feet. Out on the town celebrating her promotion, Alison meets and has a one-night-stand with Ben. The next day she realizes her mistake and ends their relationship. There's just one minor detail – she later discovers she's pregnant with Ben's child. In an effort to do what's right for their baby, Alison and Ben become a couple. What follows is a comedy about commitment, responsibility, and the realization that life doesn't care about the plans that you make.

Discussion Questions

1. **Use uncertainty reduction theory to analyze conversations between Alison and Ben as they get to know each other.**

Berger contends that our motivation to reduce uncertainty about others is enhanced when there is an incentive for us to learn more about them. In the morning after their first intimate encounter, Ben and Alison get to know each other over breakfast. Ben clearly desires another date with Alison – his motivation is high. She, on the other hand, does not share Ben's enthusiasm. A number of Berger's axioms help to analyze this scene:

Axiom 1 Verbal Communication – As verbal communication increases uncertainty decreases
Unfortunately for Ben, this axiom does not work in his favor. The more information Alison learns about his lifestyle and background, the more certain she becomes that Ben is not the guy for her. For example, Ben discloses that he is an illegal alien, he does not have a real job, and he can barely remember anything about Alison from the night before – not exactly a rewarding conversation for Alison.

Axiom 2 Nonverbal Warmth – As nonverbal expressiveness increases, uncertainty decreases
As Ben discloses more and more information about his lifestyle, Alison's grimacing and pained expressions suggest that her uncertainty is decreasing. If Ben were paying attention, he would notice that he is making Alison less likely to want to continue their relationship.

Axiom 6 Similarity – Similarities reduce uncertainty while dissimilarities increase uncertainty
Much dissimilarity exists between them: she is employed, he is not; he smokes marijuana, she does not; she is financially stable, he is not. Ben also insults Alison's profession, and this creates even more dissimilarities. Having little in common creates too many questions about Ben, and convinces Alison not to pursue a relationship with him.

Axiom 7 Liking – Increased uncertainty decreases liking; decreased uncertainty increases liking
Contrary to Berger's prediction, the more Alison gets to know Ben, the less she likes him.

The above examples can also be used to debate the usefulness of Berger's theory. For instance, is predicted outcome value (i.e., rewards versus costs of the relationship) more influential than reducing uncertainty? Alison does learn much about Ben in their initial interaction, but the costs of continuing the relationship seem to outweigh the importance of reducing uncertainty and predicting Ben's actions. Secondly, is uncertainty reduction only useful for initial interactions and first impressions? Even though their first conversation (i.e., experimenting stage) went dreadfully wrong for Ben, over time Alison learns more about Ben and eventually falls in love with him.

2. **Apply Knapp's stages of development and decline to the relationship between Alison and Ben.**

Judging by the outcome of their experimenting stage, most viewers would agree that the relationship between Ben and Alison had ended. The motivation to continue the relationship increases, however, when Alison learns that she is pregnant with Ben's child. Alison decides to go forward with her pregnancy, and she and Ben begin dating. Because their relationship is forced upon them, it's no surprise that their experimenting stage seems less about feelings of euphoria and more about feeling each other out. As uncertainty reduction predicts, Ben's use of humor and his trustworthy demeanor help to reassure Alison about their relationship. This example could also prompt discussion about what women and men are looking for in a long-term relationship. As they move into the integrating stage, Ben and Alison do more activities together (e.g., Ben helps Alison choose a gynecologist and she helps him with his job), spend more time away from their friends, and eventually see themselves as a couple. Ben attempts to move to the bonding stage when he proposes to Alison – an example of extreme symbolic commitment since Ben cannot afford a ring.

As Alison and Ben continue to get to know each other, signs of differentiating and circumscribing occur. Alison learns how Ben really feels about long-term relationships and commitment, and the inevitable stress and circumstances of Alison's pregnancy cause conflict. A significant moment of disillusionment takes place for Alison when, in the aftermath of an earthquake, she discovers that Ben never opened the baby books he promised to read. Alison interprets his behavior as a lack of commitment and the couple moves toward the stages of stagnation and avoidance. At a birthday party Alison tells Ben that they are not right for each other, and their relationship enters the terminating stage. In an effort to repair their relationship, Ben gets a job and his own apartment. When the baby is born Alison witnesses Ben's newfound commitment, and the audience is led to believe that their relationship has been repaired.

3. Which relational dialectics are Debbie and Pete experiencing? How are they choosing to manage their dialectics?

In contrast to Alison and Ben, Debbie and Pete have a longstanding romantic relationship. Indeed, they have reached a stage in their 10-year marriage where being apart is becoming more attractive than being together, at least for Pete. In other words, they are experiencing both the predictability – novelty and connection – autonomy dialectics.

During a dinner scene with Alison and Debbie, both Pete and Ben express the pitfalls of relational commitment. In their minds, being in a stable relationship automatically means losing all sense of novelty. Life simply becomes too predictable. Pete laments that he'll never be able to "drop everything and move to India," while Ben recounts visions of "driving to and breaking through the border of freedom." Their mutual solution to these feelings of helplessness and disorientation is to go back in time and change the future, rather than accept their present relationships. Their lack of sensitivity leaves Alison and Debbie at a loss for words.

Another scene illustrates the connection – autonomy dialectic. Later in the film Debbie becomes suspicious of Pete's behavior: he frequently works at odd hours of the day and is unreachable by cell phone. Debbie installs PC tracking software to monitor his electronic communication and she comes to the conclusion that Pete is cheating on her. Debbie, Alison, and Ben follow Pete to a stranger's house, expecting to catch him in the act. Instead, Debbie finds Pete in the middle of a fantasy baseball meeting. When she demands justification for his behavior, Pete explains that he secretly does these things, including going to the movies by himself, because he "needs time to himself or else he would go insane." As relational dialectics theory suggests, Debbie argues that she also desires moments of autonomy, along with dates with Pete – she is using the balance strategy. Unfortunately, Pete seems completely oblivious to both Debbie's needs and to the realization that his behavior is even a problem – he has chosen to manage this dialectic through the strategy of denial. Their conflict ends abruptly with Debbie ordering Pete to get out of the house.

Both of these scenes illustrate typical relational dialectics, and do so in a relatable way for students. Incidentally, both examples are also manageable stand-alone scenes for classroom viewing.

4. What gendered language differences are present in the conversations among Alison, Ben, Debbie, and Pete?

A number of moments in the film support research on gendered language differences. For example, talk between Ben and Pete is consistently, and almost exclusively, focused on humor and making jokes. The primary purpose of their talk is to tease one another and have fun. In fact, Ben seems particularly attracted to Pete because of how funny he is. For Alison and Debbie, their discussions primarily consist of relational topics: they talk about their relationships with Ben and Pete, about Debbie's children, and about their personal problems.

When these two styles come into contact with each other, misunderstandings occur. For instance, at one point Debbie is online searching for convicted sex offenders who live in her area. When she tries to explain her concern to Pete, he makes a joke and dismisses her anxiety as over-parenting. Debbie interprets his cavalier approach to mean that he doesn't care about their family – her constitutive meaning for his behavior. In the previously mentioned dinner scene, Ben and Pete continually make jokes about wanting to leave their relationships with Alison and Debbie. At one moment Alison seems so confused about what the men are saying, it's as if they are speaking another language entirely.

Viewing these scenes should spark discussion among students regarding their own gendered language experiences.

LARS AND THE REAL GIRL

Film Data
Year: 2007
Director: Craig Gillespie
Length: 106 Minutes
Rated: PG-13

Characters/Actors
Lars: Ryan Gosling
Karin: Emily Mortimer
Gus: Paul Schneider
Dr. Dagmar: Patricia Clarkson
Margo: Kelli Garner

Communication Courses
Communication Theory
Interpersonal Communication

Communication Concepts
Coordinated Management of Meaning Theory
Relational Dialectics
Relationship Stages
Symbolic Interactionism Theory

Pedagogical Perspective

Lars the Real Girl is the story of a man coming to grips with his identity, and a community of people supporting him. This is a quiet film, and some students may be put off initially by its slow pace. However, the film clearly illustrates interpersonal relationships and the social construction of reality through communication. *Lars and the Real Girl* is rated PG-13 for some sex-related content.

Synopsis

Lars Lindstrom is a shy, sweet man who lives by himself in his brother's garage. When Lars brings his new girlfriend (Bianca) home to meet his brother (Gus) and sister-in-law (Karin), they are thrilled – until they learn that she is an anatomically correct mannequin. At the urging of their family doctor, Gus and Karin go along with Lars' delusion. Eventually, the whole town treats Lars and Bianca as if their relationship is real. The film shows how an entire community can come together to support one individual, and how communication works to create our reality.

Discussion Questions

1. **Do Lars and Bianca have a 'real' interpersonal relationship?**

At first glance, the answer to this question seems to be "no." The term "interpersonal" characterizes communication between at least two persons. Nonetheless, Lars' one-sided 'conversations' with Bianca do fit many characteristics of qualitatively interpersonal relationships. Their relationship contains elements of intimacy, self-disclosure, relational dialectics, and conflict (See below for specific examples).

2. **Apply Knapp's stages of development and decline to the relationship between Lars and Bianca.**

During dinner at Gus and Karin's house, Lars and Bianca already seem to be moving beyond Knapp's experimenting stage toward intensifying. Apparently they already know much about each other; they sit in close proximity to one another, and frequently have quiet 'conversations'. On the way to Dr. Dagmar's office, Lars discloses to Bianca interesting tidbits about the town and his family background. Karin even gets caught up in the moment and shares details about her work, followed by a glare from Gus. Later, Lars takes Bianca to a lake where he and Gus used to play as children, because he wants Bianca to know more about himself. As they move toward the integrating stage, Lars and Bianca share many activities as a couple: they go shopping together, to church, and to parties. A close observation of Lars' cubicle at work also shows an increase in relational artifacts (pictures), again demonstrating his relationship with Bianca. In the eyes of the community, their relationship is real.

Lars and Bianca also demonstrate Knapp's coming apart stages. The first sign of differentiating is a conflict they have about Bianca's busy schedule. According to Lars, Bianca is spending too much time away from him; Bianca volunteers at the local hospital, she works part time as a mannequin, and she is a school board member. In other words, they are experiencing the connection versus autonomy dialectic. Lars denies that Bianca needs moments apart from him, and instead he believes that Bianca should be available (i.e., connected) to him at all times. Only later does Lars reveal to Dr. Dagmar the true source of his frustrations: he asked Bianca to marry him, and she said no. Her rejection seems to fuel Lars' advancement toward the circumscribing stage, as shown by his bowling 'date' with Margo. Even though Lars tells Margo that he is committed to Bianca and "would never cheat on her," obviously their relationship is in decline. Shortly thereafter, Lars terminates his relationship with Bianca by performing the script of her death.

It is important to notice that even though Lars has never had a 'real' girlfriend, he performs the roles of intimacy rather well. Each of these examples shows how relationships, although unique, can also be predictable and scripted.

3. **Using symbolic interactionism theory (meaning, language, and thought), describe how the characters co-construct their reality through communication. How does the community of townspeople, the generalized other, contribute to the film's narrative?**

The film offers examples of Mead's symbolic interactionism theory, including his central concepts of meaning, language, and thought. Mead theorized that we are all social actors, co-creating our meanings through communication. Language, the source of meaning, both clarifies and constrains what we call reality. How we label a person, a relationship, an event, influences how we act toward these phenomena. And there lies the central paradox of the film: In order for Lars to improve his mental state, all of the other characters have to act as if his relationship with Bianca is real, even if she is not. Surprisingly, the characters adapt rather quickly.

When Lars first introduces Bianca to Gus and Karin, they are, naturally, at a loss for words. Gus immediately calls his brother "insane" and "crazy," and treats Lars as such. During his conversation with Dr. Dagmar, Gus is mostly concerned with "fixing" Lars and worried about "what people [the generalized other] will think." At one point Gus unsuccessfully attempts to shock Lars out of his delusion by calling Bianca a "plastic thing." Only after Dr. Dagmar reminds Gus that Bianca is 'real' to Lars, Gus begins to treat the relationship as real. Somewhat grudgingly he does take care of Bianca, driving her around, putting her to bed, even going so far as to bathe her. For Gus, Lars' relationship with Bianca becomes a way for him to deal with his guilt over leaving Lars alone with their father.

Karin also views Lars' relationship with Bianca as "odd," though she is more understanding than Gus. During their first dinner Karin serves food to Bianca, and reluctantly allows Bianca to borrow her clothes. Because Karin had an uncle who was sent away to a mental institution, she has a different meaning for Lars' behavior. Later in an emotional scene with Lars, Karin explains to him that she takes care of Bianca, and the entire town takes care of Bianca, because they love Lars – that is the meaning of their actions.

The townspeople (Mead's "generalized other") also co-create Lars and Bianca's relationship. When the news about Lars travels around town, once again the characters attach different meanings to the situation: Gus' co-workers chide him, Karin's friends are in disbelief about "sex dolls" even existing, and members of the church are angry. These meanings take an abrupt shift when Lars brings Bianca to a party. Of particular note are the gender roles that play out, even though the characters know Bianca is not real. For example, some of the women sit around debating whether Lars would allow Bianca to change her hair, while Lars' male friends comment on her physical appearance and "flexibility." Eventually, Bianca becomes ingrained in the community, volunteering at the hospital and serving on the school board. When Bianca becomes ill and ultimately 'dies,' the community shows their support through a variety of symbols: cards, flowers, and the funeral.

Using symbolic interactionism theory to analyze the situation reminds us how powerful communication can be to create our reality.

4. Apply CMM theory to the film by explaining the regulative and constitutive rules the characters follow, including both coordinated and uncoordinated meanings.

Similar to symbolic interactionism theory, CMM theorists argue that through communication we create our reality. In addition, CMM calls our attention to rules, regulative and constitutive, that help us to coordinate our actions with others.

One obvious example of an uncoordinated conversation is the aforementioned dinner among Lars, Bianca, Karin, and Gus. Typically, as CMM predicts, episodes such as 'having dinner' are rather scripted. Implied regulative rules guide our actions: polite conversations transpire between the hosts and guests, the depth of self-disclosure is usually kept to a minimum, and food is consumed for the purpose of getting to know each other. When Lars introduces Bianca to Karin and Gus, naturally they have difficulty coordinating this episode. Still, regulative rules are powerful, as evidenced by Karin offering a plate of food to Bianca. Later in their car ride to see Dr. Dagmar, Karin again follows the regulative rule of polite conversation when she tells Bianca about her job. Eventually, the entire town coordinates their actions together to create the reality of Lars' relationship with Bianca.

Concerning constitutive rules, the meanings we attach to our actions and the actions of others, a great example is Karin's heated argument with Lars. Karin explains to Lars that the reason she and Gus take care of Bianca, that the entire town takes care of Bianca, is because they love him. This is the constitutive meaning of their actions – doing things for Bianca is a sign of love for Lars. It appears that once he accepts that he is capable of being loved, Lars no longer needs his relationship with Bianca.

Certainly there are additional applications of CMM theory in the film. For students struggling to understand this complicated theory, these scenes should be beneficial.

THE LAST KISS

Film Data

Year: 2006
Director: Tony Goldwyn
Length: 104 Minutes
Rated: R

Characters/Actors

Michael: Zach Braff
Jenna: Jacinda Barrett
Kim: Rachel Bilson
Chris: Casey Affleck
Izzy: Michael Weston
Kenny: Eric Christian Olsen
Anna: Blythe Danner
Stephen: Tom Wilkinson

Communication Courses

Communication Theory
Interpersonal Communication

Communication Concepts

Deception
Relational Dialectics
Self-Disclosure and Emotional Expression

Pedagogical Perspective

The Last Kiss is certainly not the feel-good romantic-comedy of any film season. Still, it investigates topics that are familiar to students, and leaves plenty of opportunity for debate about philosophies of relationships (e.g., Is honesty always the best policy? Can broken trust ever be forgiven? Should friends lie for one anther?). And even though the storyline revolves around post-college adulthood, themes of commitment, friendship, and trust will resonate with college-age students. A class might also use the film to explore differences in relational expectations between men and women, and how those expectations are expressed. The film is rated R for several scenes of nudity and sex, so one should be advised before showing the entire film to a classroom audience.

Synopsis

Michael (Braff) seems to have it all: a beautiful girlfriend (Barrett) who clearly loves him, a stable career as an architect, and the closeness that only a group of long-term friends can provide. Indeed, he has everything he ever dreamed for – and that is his dilemma. When Jenna announces that she is pregnant and starts talking about marriage and buying a house, Michael wonders if life as he knows it is now over. He begins to question his commitment to Jenna. That commitment is tested when Michael meets Kim (Bilson) at the wedding of a mutual friend. Kim's free-spirited persona and attractive appearance tempt Michael, and he ends up cheating on Jenna. What results is a series of lies perpetuated by Michael, Jenna's discovery of these lies and his infidelity, and Michael's attempts to repair their relationship.

Incidentally, Michael and Jenna are not the only characters in the film suffering from relational discord. Michael's friend Izzy (Weston) can't seem to let go of a past relationship, driving him to near depression. Another friend, Chris (Affleck), constantly argues with his neurotic wife about taking care of their newborn child, prompting him to suggest that they split up. And Jenna's parents, Anna (Danner) and Stephen (Wilkinson), are going through their own discovery of infidelity after thirty years of marriage.

Discussion Questions

1. **Describe the dialectical tensions Michael is experiencing in his relationship with Jenna, and how he chooses to manage those tensions.**

In the beginning of the film Michael and Jenna appear to be a happy couple. When the audience witnesses the announcement to Jenna's parents that a baby is on the way, however, we soon learn that Michael is struggling with relational commitment and the predictability/novelty relational dialectic. On the one hand, Michael comments that he always dreamed that his life would turn out this way: stable employment, loving relationship, a child on the way, etc. In other words, it's all been very predictable. However, now that he has what he's always dreamed for, he wonders if there's anything left (novelty). Unfortunately Michael chooses to manage his dialectical tension with the disorientation response. When he meets Kim at the wedding, he discovers in her the novelty that he desires. They go on a date, eventually engage in sexual intercourse, and Michael realizes the grave mistake he has made.

2. **How do Michael and Jenna talk about their relational expectancies through self-disclosure and emotional expression?**

Early in the film, Jenna asks Michael very directly if he is committed to the relationship, if he is ready for the responsibilities of a baby. Instead of honestly expressing his fears and anxiety to Jenna, Michael chooses to keep his true emotions to himself. He lies, and says everything is okay. Later, he becomes overwhelmed with the perceived certainty of his future and instead of talking about this with Jenna, he has the affair with Kim. Sadly, only after Jenna learns of Michael's affair do they finally engage in appropriate self-disclosure and emotional expression about their relational expectations. Now Michael expresses how terrified he is about having the baby, and Jenna confirms that she shares his feelings. Perhaps feeling overly confident and that this honesty thing is pretty good, Michael then discloses that indeed he did have sex with Kim. Jenna becomes violent and storms out of the room, illustrating that honesty is conditional.

3. **What verbal and nonverbal cues give Michael away when he lies to Chris? What cues give Chris away when he lies to Jenna? How does Jenna's suspicion affect the outcome?**

The film also provides many examples of verbal and nonverbal cues that accompany Michael's deceit. When he lies to Chris about covering for him with Jenna, Michael's brief and vague responses to Chris's questions are excellent examples of leakage. Michael also alters this tone of voice and avoids direct eye contact with Chris. Because Chris knows Michael so well, these violations of Michael's typical conversational style are easy indicators for Chris that he his lying.

Even though Chris easily spots Michael's deception, he is equally a poor liar when Jenna confronts him about Michael's whereabouts. In their scene Chris immediately provides the answer to a question Jenna did not ask, when he blurts out "Michael's not here." As Jenna's suspicion increases along with the veracity of her probing, Chris stumbles and stutters his way to an answer, ultimately confessing that he has no idea where Michael is. Both scenes illustrate the interactive nature of deception, cues that give liars away, and how suspicion influences the entire sequence.

4. What are the consequences of deception presented in the film?

When Jenna discovers Michael's deceit, she struggles to forgive him and their relationship appears to be in serious doubt; this agrees with most research on the topic. Yet the final scene of the film, when Jenna lets Michael back into the house, suggests that she will forgive him. Is this realistic? Jenna's parents, Anna (Blythe Danner) and Stephen (Tom Wilkinson), also struggle with their own discovery of unfaithfulness. Unlike his daughter's emotional outburst, however, Stephen seems to forgive Anna's indiscretion in a surprisingly calm manner. Is this realistic?

LITTLE MISS SUNSHINE

Film Data
Year: 2006
Directors: Valerie Faris, Jonathan Dayton
Length: 101 minutes
Rated: R

Characters/Actors
Olive: Abigail Breslin
Richard: Greg Kinnear
Dwayne: Paul Dano
Grandpa: Alan Arkin
Sheryl: Toni Collette
Frank: Steve Carell

Communication Courses
Family Communication
Group Communication
Interpersonal Communication

Communication Concepts
Confirming/Disconfirming Communication
Family Communication
Self-Concept Formation
Self-Disclosure

Pedagogical Perspective

This heart-warming, popular film first strikes most viewers with the sheer dysfunction of its family members; but the hilarity of the situations coupled with the personal growth of its characters increases its applicability to interpersonal communication concepts.

Synopsis

Little Miss Sunshine chronicles the adventures of 7-year old Olive (Breslin) and her dysfunctional family as they travel from New Mexico to California, where Olive is to compete in the Little Miss Sunshine beauty contest.

Olive's relatives are so burdened with their own quirks and neuroses that making it to California sane, alive and on time for the pageant is uncertain until the end of the film. From tensions revealed early in the movie (i.e., the explosive dinner scene), it's clear that the 800-mile journey could do irreparable harm to each family member, and to all of their strained relationships. Along the way, the Hoover family members experience profound changes, individually and collectively, as they all begin to share closely held personal secrets and experiences—and in so doing grow closer.

Discussion Questions

1. Describe the disconfirming messages presented by the various characters in the film.

Olive's father Richard (Kinnear) unrelentingly pitches his nine-step self-help program considering how the characters, who are struggling with problems (and thus may have good reason to feel like losers) may receive his comments. Particularly disconfirming is his lecture to his suicidal brother-in-law about those who "refuse to lose." Richard's communication with his family members is typically tangential, interrupting, and especially impersonal, each sending a non-valuing message. As Richard is being pulled over by the police, he yells out to his passengers, "Everyone, just, pretend to be normal."

Other disconfirming messages are sent by teenage son Dwayne (Dano) who is obsessed with Friederich Nietzsche and hasn't spoken a word in nine months as a protest to living with the family he claims to detest. Along with his silence, Dwayne periodically scribbles "I hate everyone" or "Welcome to hell" on the pad of paper that is his only means of verbal communication.

Additional disconfirming messages are sent by Grandpa as he mocks Richard and criticizes his life's work. Grandpa also complains a lot, about everything from the pains of aging to eating chicken for dinner too often. Once the family reaches the pageant, pageant officials send numerous disconfirming messages to Olive and her family. During the pageant's talent competition, Pageant Official Jenkins rolls her eyes, gasps audibly, and asks Olive's father Richard what Olive's doing, all signaling her disapproval of Olive and her chosen talent routine. Following Olive's act, the pageant officials ask security personnel to intervene, making the Hoover family agree to "never enter your daughter in a beauty pageant in the state of California ever again." Clearly, these messages are a far cry from endorsements or a valued and confirming response.

2. Describe the confirming messages presented by Sheryl in the film.

Despite the family's perpetual financial crisis, Olive's mother Sheryl (Collette) works hard to avoid threatening the face of other family members. She takes care of her suicidal brother Frank (Carrel), is unremittingly kind to her hostile son Dwayne, supportive of her husband Richard in the face of his business failures, and patient with her crude father in law (Arkin). And she constantly supports and encourages Olive's dream of becoming a beauty queen along with the other family members to pursue their goals, dreams and needed healing throughout the film.

3. Describe how the characters disclose personal information throughout the trip and how that disclosure enhances their relationships.

The grandfather is unabashedly disclosive. He explains to 7-year-old Olive that her Uncle Frank tried to kill himself, talks freely about his sexually promiscuous past, and calls upon the others in the van to be real about what's upsetting them. As they travel, Uncle Frank begins to disclose the truth about his failed romantic relationship and career. Once his book deal has fallen through, father Richard breaks down and begins to share his feelings of failure and disappointment after years of spouting the same self-help "be a winner" messages. Upon realizing he won't be able to achieve his career dream of becoming a fighter pilot, Son Dwayne begins to disclose his feelings and disappointment. All of these revelations make the vulnerable individuals interact directly with each other, drawing the characters closer as a group.

4. How did the family members bond and find a sense of cohesiveness in the 800-mile journey?

There are several examples of the family growing more cohesive by working together in the face of challenges. The most visually memorable example occurs each time the family must give their aging Volkswagen van a running push every time they start. The family also unites to deal with a surprising medical event that puts grandpa in an Arizona hospital. Another amusing example of family cohesiveness occurs when the parents and brother Dwayne unite to support sister Olive's unique performance in the beauty contest talent show.

5. Describe Olive's self concept and body image.

Bespectacled, chubby Olive dreams of becoming Little Miss Sunshine, and focuses her time and energy on this goal. While Olive has an adorable personality, her self-appraisal as a potential child beauty queen probably isn't very realistic. Nonetheless, no one in the family tells her that she isn't pretty enough, although several express concerns about Olive getting her feelings hurt when she doesn't win. In one scene, Olive starts to realize that she may not be as good-looking as she thought. She asks her grandpa, "Am I pretty?" He lovingly replies that she's the "most beautiful girl in the world." In another scene, Richard seems to be trying to discourage Olive from pursuing the pageant further by lecturing once again about the natures of winners and losers, but his ambiguity and redundancy fall short of making his point of her likely failure in the pageant with her. Later, when at a restaurant with the whole family, Richard more candidly and concretely cautions the somewhat chubby 7-year-old of the dangers of eating too much ice cream if she wants to keep entering beauty pageants. The rest of the family dismisses his criticisms as they dance around the issue of Olive's body image. Once at the pageant, it's especially clear to the family members that Olive looks very different from the other contestants and they try to leave before she performs, to help her avoid the likely painful rejection.

OFFICE SPACE

Film Data
Year: 1999
Director: Mike Judge
Length: 88 minutes
Rated: R

Characters/Actors
Peter Gibbons: Ron Livingston
Joanna: Jennifer Aniston
Milton: Stephen Root
Samir: Ajay Naidu
Michael Bolton: David Herman
Bill Lumbergh: Gary Cole

Communication Courses
Interpersonal Communication
Organizational Communication

Communication Concepts
Classical Theory/Theory X
Communication Climate
Conflict
Honesty/Lying
Language
Self-Concept/Identity Management

Pedagogical Perspective

The back cover of the *Office Space* video proudly announces that the film is by Mike Judge, creator of *Beavis and Butt-head*, which should serve warning that the movie has some crude content and language (as well as two brief sexual scenes). While this is a very humorous film, it touches on some serious issues that can be explored. (For example, see "Investigating the Relationship Between Superior-Subordinate Relationship Quality and Employee Dissent" by J. W. Kassing in *Communication Research Reports* (2000), Vol. 17, pp. 58–69).

One of the unstated morals of *Office Space* is that Peter's life becomes better when he stops closely managing his identity and begins doing and saying whatever he wants. While this makes for an entertaining movie (and is the premise for other entertaining films such as *Liar Liar*), the outcomes of Peter's decisions can and should be a point of discussion for communication students. Would Peter actually be promoted to management if he ignored his boss, came to work whenever he wanted, dressed in shorts, destroyed company property, and admitted his lack of motivation to outside consultants? Probably only in Hollywood, which makes this a good case study for debating the pros and cons of identity management, honesty, and rhetorical sensitivity in the workplace.

Synopsis

Peter Gibbons (Livingston) and his colleagues Samir (Naidu) and Michael (Herman) are computer specialists who are fed up with their mundane jobs. They work at Initech Corporation, an impersonal organization with a Classical Theory/Theory X approach to management. Their boss Lumbergh (Cole) has a condescending attitude and creates a defensive communication climate with all employees, including Milton (Root), the emotionally challenged mailroom clerk who keeps threatening to "burn the building." In a hypnotherapy session, Peter loses his inhibitions and starts speaking his mind around the office. His "straight shooting" earns him a promotion while others are downsized out of the company. Peter and his colleagues carry out a high-tech embezzling scheme to get revenge on Initech. Peter's new girlfriend Joanna (Aniston) is also fed up with her waitress job and her manager; however, she helps Peter realize that embezzling is an unethical way to handle his frustration with Initech. Ultimately, Peter and his friends move on to new horizons and Initech (quite literally) goes up in flames.

Discussion Questions

1. **Describe how the Initech Corporation illustrates Classical Theory and Theory X approaches to organizational communication.**

Initech embodies the worst features of a classical style of management. It is a hierarchy with centralized organizational power in which non-managers have little or no participation in decisions that affect their lives and their productivity. For example, a large overhead banner at a staff meeting reads, "Is this good for the company?" At this meeting, Lumbergh announces that outside consultants have been hired to assess the company's needs. The nonverbal responses of the employees clearly show they fear the worst about their jobs and their futures. Rather than acknowledging their downcast expressions, Lumbergh changes the subject (disconfirmation) and announces that "next Friday will be Hawaiian shirt day!" The company is highly impersonal but attempts to keep up a facade of being "employee oriented" with gimmicks such as banners, Hawaiian shirt days, and birthday parties (which employees attend with little enthusiasm).

In the tradition of McGregor's Theory X, the upper-level management assumes that a strong and forceful hand is essential for harnessing the efforts of basically unmotivated employees. For instance, Peter hears from three different bosses about his incorrect TPS reports—and in each case, the bosses pay no attention to Peter's explanation. Initech managers and consultants make decisions for rather than with the employees, including decisions that eliminate talented (but underutilized) workers. As a result of feeling unvalued, the employees do as little work as possible, watch the clock, and try to appear busy when the bosses are watching. Without personal, professional, or monetary incentives to perform well, the employees view their jobs as a prison sentence they must serve until they retire or are fired.

2. **Describe the communication climate in manager-employee interactions in the movie.**

The Initech managers create negative communication climates with the employees they oversee. In terms of Gibb's climate categories, Lumbergh uses a variety of defense-arousing behaviors. He has an attitude of superiority and is evaluative, controlling, and strategic in his interactions. For example, Peter arrives at work on Monday morning and Lumbergh stops by to say, "What's happening?" It is a counterfeit question, since he is not really interested in Peter's response. Lumbergh's intent is to confront Peter about a mistake in his TPS report. Lumbergh gives Peter a patronizing lecture that ends with, "If you could go ahead and make sure to do that from now on, that would be great" (a comment that might be appropriate if it had been part of a problem-solving dialogue rather than a fault-finding monologue). Lumbergh says he will re-send the memo; Peter holds up a copy and declares, "I already have the memo!" Lumbergh disconfirms Peter by ignoring him and walking away. A few minutes later, Peter is reprimanded by several other bosses about the same TPS report—and they all deliver the message in a condescending tone.

At five o'clock on a Friday afternoon, Lumbergh approaches Peter and tells him (rather than asks him) to work on Saturday and Sunday. Lumbergh creates an environment of control and neutrality as he shows no respect or regard for other plans that Peter may have made for his weekend. Lumbergh is also indifferent and callous with Milton (the mailroom clerk) when he moves Milton's cubicle numerous times, speaks negatively about him in front of others, and gives him the job of "working on the roach problem." The irony is that all of Lumbergh's negative messages come out of his mouth in a calm, syrupy tone of voice—as if he had been taught to speak this way at a management-training seminar. Rather than having a calming effect, his patronizing vocalics and expressions provoke defensiveness.

Even the consultants' recommendation to fire Milton by simply stopping his paychecks demonstrates the Gibb components of strategy, neutrality, and control. They declare that Milton will eventually figure out that he is no longer employed, and thus the problem "will sort itself out." Until then, Milton dangles in the wind, wondering why he has been moved to the basement and isn't getting paid. The consultants acknowledge their preference for hiding bad news when they admit to Peter that "it's better to fire people on a Friday—statistical studies show that there is less chance of an incident if you do it at the end of the week."

Peter's girlfriend Joanna is a waitress who experiences similar frustrations with her restaurant manager. His messages, both verbal and nonverbal, create a negative communication climate. He is ambiguous and indirect as he talks to her about her lack of "flair" (a euphemism meant to describe the attitude and environment of fun at the restaurant—but something that he measures by the number of buttons she wears on her uniform). He talks down to her, rolls his eyes, and asks Joanna counterfeit, impersonal questions such as "What do you think of a person that only does the bare minimum?" He also sends her a mixed message by telling her, "Some people choose to wear more [flair buttons]; you do want to express yourself don't you?"—when in fact he is telling her that he doesn't like the way she has chosen to express herself. (Note: This scene is discussed in detail in Section II)

Euphemisms and vagueness are part of the Initech culture as well—which contribute to the employees feeling defensive around the managers. As mentioned above, the workers learn that when Lumbergh asks, "What's happening?" he really means, "I'm checking up on you" or "I have bad news to deliver." Lumbergh's instructions about time sheets are indecipherable—the employees are clearly lost, but no one speaks up. The more obscure his language, the less his employees want to challenge his instructions.

3. What styles of conflict management are used by the managers and employees in the movie?

Peter's initial style of conflict management with his managers is non-assertion. He tries to accommodate the bosses when they confront him about his TPS reports, saying he will "correct the mistake; there isn't a problem." Peter avoids confrontation with Lumbergh, going so far as to hide in his cubicle to keep from interacting with him. When Lumbergh tells him to come to work over the weekend, Peter says nothing and accepts Lumbergh's orders.

After hypnotherapy, Peter becomes assertive with his boss. When Lumbergh begins to talk to him, Peter walks by as if Lumbergh isn't there. In another scene, Peter sees Lumbergh approaching and says, "Not now Lumbergh—I have a meeting with the consultants." Emboldened by Peter's new style, his fellow employees begin to handle their conflicts through indirect and direct aggression—and in ways that interpersonal textbooks describe as dysfunctional (i.e., isolation, escalation, shortsightedness). They embezzle funds from Initech, then take a computer from the company to an outdoor field and bash it to pieces. Milton, who early in the movie handles his conflict by mumbling his dissatisfaction under his breath, takes out his anger on Initech by burning down the office building.

Joanna's conflict style changes from nonassertion to direct aggression in her interactions with her boss. Initially she tries to understand and clarify what the boss wants from her by asking, "So you want me to wear more pieces of flair?" In a later scene, when her boss is attacking her again for her lack of flair, Joanna says, "If you want me to wear 37 pieces of flair, why don't you make the minimum 37 pieces of flair?" Then she adds, "Do you want me to express myself?" (as she holds up her middle finger). She loudly exclaims, "This is me expressing myself … I hate this job and I don't need it!"

4. Describe the changes Peter experiences in his identity management.

Peter demonstrates careful identity management early in the movie by maintaining the image of a dedicated, hard-working employee—despite the disdain he holds for the company and his job. He adapts his communication to the role he plays and the environment he is in. He is well groomed, wears a suit and tie, and calmly tries to do "what is good for the company." In the scene when Lumbergh confronts Peter about the mistake with the TPS reports, Peter maintains a "good employee" facade despite the fact that he is furious inside. Peter later reveals his job frustration to a hypnotherapist and says, "Every day is the worst day of my life."

After Peter's hypnotherapy, he adopts a relaxed, "I don't care" attitude. He does not work during the weekend as requested by Lumbergh. He rolls out of bed at his convenience, dresses in shorts and a t-shirt, and leisurely strolls into the office late on Monday. Peter arrives just in time for his interview with the consultants and tells them exactly what is on his mind, with no attempt to manage his employee identity (he admits, "I just don't care. Where is the motivation?"). Peter takes apart his cubicle to have an open view out the window and cleans a fish on his desk in front of Lumbergh. When Lumbergh attempts to confront him, Peter simply brushes him off.

Peter's newfound freedom from the strictures of identity management leads to changes in his personal life as well. He visits Chotchkie's restaurant to see Joanna (whom he has admired from afar) and tells her outright, "I don't like my job and I'm not going anymore." When she asks what he wants to do, he responds, "Take you out to dinner and go back to my apartment to watch Kung Fu." She finds his honesty (and love of Kung Fu) refreshing and the two of them strike up a relationship.

Peter's trance-like state from the hypnotist slowly fades, but he retains his new perspective and assertive approach to life. After Peter confesses about and attempts to return the embezzled money to Initech, he is ready to face the consequences of his actions. When he arrives at work, he discovers that Initech is burning to the ground and that his embezzling scheme will remain a secret. Peter moves on to a manual labor job where he receives more intrinsic rewards for his work—and where he needs to be far less concerned about managing his identity.

OUTSOURCED

Film Data
Year: 2006
Director: John Jeffcoat
Length: 103 Minutes
Rated: PG-13

Characters/Actors
Todd Anderson: Josh Hamilton
Asha: Ayesha Dharker
Puro: Asif Basra
Dave: Matt Smith

Communication Courses
Business Communication
Intercultural Communication
Organizational Communication

Communication Concepts
Adapting to Diversity
Culture Shock
Individualism and Collectivism
Organizational Culture
Proxemics

Pedagogical Perspective

Outsourced is an independent film that students likely have not seen, though critics have taken notice of it. The film is equally useful for illustrating intercultural situations and business communication. Likewise, instructors could show the film in its entirety, or select clips to demonstrate concepts. *Outsourced* is rated PG-13 for some sex-related content.

Synopsis

So far, the life of Todd Anderson has been predictable and uneventful. He manages a customer service call center in Seattle, for a company selling novelty products. However, his world is turned upside down when his job, and everyone under him, is outsourced to India. If being fired weren't bad enough, Todd's boss strong-arms him into going to India to train his replacement. In India Todd is overwhelmed by the cultural differences, both in and out of the new call center. He eventually finds a way to train his new staff and increase their productivity, but not before Todd learns something about himself.

Discussion Questions

1. **Identify examples of Todd's culture shock, including his loss of personal space. Also, apply Edward Hall's distances in your explanation.**

Culture shock is generally recognized as feelings of discomfort, disorientation, and helplessness for individuals traveling abroad. When Todd steps off his plane in Bombay, he immediately experiences culture shock. Viewers witness Todd's wide-eyed stairs into the sea of arriving people, his inability to accomplish routine tasks (e.g., hailing a taxi), and his reluctance at literally throwing himself into an overcrowded train. Todd realizes rather quickly that he is no longer in the United States. His assumptions of cultural similarities culminate when he mistakenly drinks a local beverage that makes him very ill, and he nearly insults the "schmuck" whom he has been sent to train. Eventually Todd's culture shock subsides, and he gradually adapts to his new surroundings (see Question 3 below).

Edward Hall identified four distances that individuals use in everyday interactions. As an American out in public, Todd is mostly used to communicating with others at range of four to twelve feet, or what Hall called social distance. Hall also argued that personal distance is set aside for more casual conversations. Intimate distance, as the name suggests, is the distance reserved for individuals who are especially important to us – certainly not the preferred distance for talking with strangers. Todd learns rather quickly that in India, in public and private, space is a luxury. For instance, the train that Todd wants to ride is so crowded that people are literally bulging out of the doors and windows. After Todd forces is way onto the train and somehow finds a seat, a young boy, a stranger, sits down on Todd's knee as if this behavior is normal. This is clearly a violation of Todd's intimate space, though it is not the last cultural violation he will experience. Later, he mistakenly eats food with his left hand, which Indians consider "unclean." If Todd wants to survive his sojourn to India, he will need to observe his new surroundings more carefully.

2. **Recognize examples of Todd's individualism and the host culture's collectivism.**

Individualistic cultures, such as the United States, place a greater emphasis on individual rights, freedoms, and expressions. Moreover, an "I" consciousness permeates conversations with others, both in public and private. In contrast, collectivistic cultures, including India, value group goals, relationships, and hierarchy – one's class rank in the social structure is especially important for Indians. Collectivism is characterized by a "we" consciousness, and a commitment to groups (e.g., family and organizations) is valued.

When Todd meets the owner of the house where he is staying (Auntie), she quickly bombards him with questions that are meant to determine his social rank. She asks him what his father does for a living, Todd's current salary, and if he is married. When Todd reveals that not only is he not married but he has recently broken up with his girlfriend, Auntie has difficulty even comprehending such a decision. In her eyes, Todd is old enough to be married with children, perhaps even grandchildren. Her comments, and disbelief, illustrate a collectivistic perspective toward family relationships and social status – being married is a symbol of success. Throughout the film, Auntie the matchmaker endeavors to find a suitable mate for Todd.

During conversations with his office assistant, Puro, Todd confesses that he rarely visits his parents even though they live two hours away. Displaying his collectivistic values, Puro cannot not understand why Todd does not still live with his parents, or at least visit them every week. Todd responds ambiguously, "It's complicated."

Later in the film Todd develops a romantic relationship with one of his employees, Asha. Because of her arranged engagement to another man, Asha's intimacy with Todd must remain a secret. At one point Todd questions Asha why such a smart and strong woman like herself would continue with the marriage in India – from Todd's individualistic perspective his point makes sense. Asha's collectivism speaks loudly when she says, "I cannot leave, I would miss my parents too much…I have obligations."

3. **Provide examples that illustrate Todd's process of adapting to cultural diversity (i.e., resistance, tolerance, understanding, respect, and participation).**

Resistance – During the first few moments of Todd's stay in India, he rejects the beliefs and practices of the host community. He is angry that he has been forced into this culture, and he often expresses to others that he cannot wait to leave. Todd also insults Indians with his ethnocentric behavior. For instance, at one point he explains to his native employees how Americans enjoy branding young cows, sacred animals in India, with a hot iron. He also makes little effort to correctly pronounce the names of his employees, and is visibly annoyed that his name when spoken sounds like "toad." Todd's frustration with Indian culture gets the best of him when he yells at Puro about the call center's poor productivity.

Tolerance – Fortunately, however, Todd's resistance is mixed with tolerance. While he may not understand or agree with many Indian practices, he does at least tolerate some of them. For example, Todd learns to avoid eating with his left hand, in deference to Indian custom. Also, poor children on the street frequently beg Todd for food and money, and one particular boy enjoys stealing Todd's cell phone – he gives the boy pens and eventually befriends him. Viewers witness Todd's obvious annoyance with these features of Indian culture, although his resistance is waning.

Understanding – Three specific moments illustrate when Todd moves from resistance/tolerance to understanding. First, in an epic search for something familiar, something that will bring him comfort, Todd takes a taxi to Bombay looking for a cheeseburger. Instead he finds a fellow American business traveler who offers him sage advice: Don't resist India, give in. Secondly, after his mindless insult of Indians' beliefs about cows, one of his employees suggests that instead of teaching them about America, Todd should learn about India. Finally, Todd reaches understanding when he accidentally leaves for work not knowing it is a special day for Indians. It is Happy Holy Day, a day to celebrate the changing of seasons. Instead of his routine walk to the call center, Todd and Puro are assaulted with water balloons and clouds of colorful powder. Todd happily joins in on the fun, and his sublime smile as he cleanses himself in a river suggests that has finally let go of his resistance.

Respect – During the film, Todd learns to place his leftover food on a wall that separates Auntie's courtyard with the surrounding community. Normally, the tray returns empty. One afternoon a flower comes back with the tray, and Todd starts to respect the kindness of Indians despite their daily struggle for survival. Later, the patriarch of a poor family invites Todd to his home for dinner – Todd literally, and symbolically, goes over the wall that separates social classes. As they all enjoy this meager meal in silence, Todd's respect for Indian generosity grows.

Participation – Once Todd lets go of his resistance and moves toward understanding/respect, he even starts adopting some Indian practices. For example, he wears traditional Indian clothing to work, and in a humorous scene he even dances like a Bollywood film character. When Todd eventually returns to the United States he brings back his newfound liking of sweet tea, as viewers watch him place four teaspoons in a single cup.

4. **Analyze the organizational culture of the call center when Todd first arrives compared to the end of the film, including their rituals and customs. How was Todd able to motivate the employees and change their organizational culture?**

Like his new cultural surroundings outside of work, Todd quickly realizes that he will need to get used to the organizational culture of the call center. When he arrives at the center, he is greeted by a mystical sign above the door that reads "Fulfilment" [sic]. Inside, few employees understand their job (one even spends most of his time flirting with female callers), and a cow is roaming freely through the offices. All around him he sees problems, in spite of everyone insisting that this is "not a problem."

Todd's initial solution to the employees' poor performance is to take an autocratic approach – he will educate them how to be American. For example, Todd tries to teach his employees to talk like Americans on the phone. His attempts are met with confusion and resistance. Rather than cultivating the relationships with his employees, Todd focuses on reducing the "bottom line." In this context success means lowering their MPI, a number referring to minutes per incident. A lower MPI is necessary for Todd to leave India, and his employees are nowhere near that goal. Puro's ineffective strategy is to plead with his workers to "please talk faster and faster, thank you."

Todd's second attempt to change the organizational culture begins with a question to the employees, "How can I improve your work life?" The employees respond with several suggestions: allow us to display photos of our family on our desks, to dress more casually, and to purchase items from the company at a discount. Todd also institutes an employee incentive plan, and it seems to work as their MPI lowers each day. Finally, Todd embraces their "not a problem" culture when a flood forces the entire call center to the roof of the building. His decision to listen to his employees, and not force them to adopt American practices, creates a productive work environment.

A completely different take on their organizational culture is to argue that if anything, Todd made the call center more like an American business, not less. Like many collectivistic cultures, India is also a culture of high power distance – organizational members readily accept and expect differences in status. In that sense, the employees should have responded better to Todd's autocratic style of leadership, not by asking for their input. Likewise, increasing motivation by allowing them to dress casually, personalize their cubicles, and compete against each other for incentives – all of these are typical American strategies for business.

THE PAINTED VEIL

Film Data
Year: 2006
Director: John Curran
Length: 125 minutes
Rated: PG-13

Characters/Actors
Kitty Fane: Naomi Watts
Walter Fane: Edward Norton
Charlie Townsend: Liev Schreiber

Communication Course
Interpersonal Communication

Communication Concepts
Confirming/Disconfirming Communication
Dialectical Tensions
Relational Stages

Pedagogical Perspective

Students may find *The Painted Veil* slow moving at first, and some may be put off that it's a period piece set primarily in China. However, the development of characters and examples of effective and ineffective interpersonal communication make this film worth the investment of time and energy.

Synopsis

The Painted Veil chronicles the tragic 1920s relationship of a young English couple. Shy bacteriologist Walter Fane (Norton) and vivacious, spirited socialite Kitty (Watts) marry after an all-too-brief courtship, and soon move to Shanghai where Walter pursues his career. Consumed by his work and socially awkward, Walter rarely listens to Kitty's words, and more importantly, to the feelings behind them. Kitty soon finds herself in an affair with witty diplomat Charlie Townsend (Schreiber) until husband Walter learns of the infidelity and vengefully forces her to travel with him to help save a war-torn village ravaged by cholera. Their cold, loveless marriage is tested in this remote and dangerous environment, and they begin to heal their relationship through listening and mutual respect.

Discussion Questions

1. Describe the disconfirming messages Walter sends to Kitty.

Early in the film, Kitty is seen chatting to Walter without much response, recognition or acknowledgement from him. In one scene, after Walter ignores her, she asks him why he didn't answer her. He replies, "I suppose I'm not used to speaking unless I've something to say." Kitty's self-disclosures are met with little or no response or nonverbal cues of encouragement. When Walter later discovers that his wife has had an affair, he withdraws further from her, only communicating in the briefest, most impersonal ways. His polite, hostile distance is far more punishing to her than any sort of visible rage.

2. Describe the relational stages in the couple's relationship.

Kitty is desperate to escape her parents' home, and Walter wants to marry before he heads to China. Despite an abbreviated period of coming together (devoid of much experimenting and even less intensifying and integrating), Walter proposes, and the relationship quickly moves to the stage of bonding. Once in China, Walter and Kitty soon discover that their relationship is coming apart. They experience differentiating, circumscribing, stagnating, and a great deal of avoiding. Before they separate and divorce, however, the couple moves to a remote cholera plagued village, where they rekindle their relationship in the face of shared adversity. As they struggle together, mutual respect and love grow. Kitty and Walter find new ways of interacting (experimenting), and as they do so their feelings for one another intensify. As the movie moves towards its dramatic conclusion, we see that this couple is truly integrated. The second life of this relationship illustrates that relational trajectories do not always move in a single direction.

3. What relational dialectics can be seen in the couple's relationship?

By temperament, Walter is fundamentally a loner who prefers autonomy, while Kitty craves connection. Nonetheless, in the latter part of the film Kitty does find strength and self-sufficiency in solitude and Walter discovers that he does want and need Kitty. If we imagine this marriage going on for decades, it's easy to imagine that the push-pull of the autonomy-connection dialectic would continue.

Another dialectical tension the couple struggles with is openness-privacy. Walter prefers privacy, whereas Kitty freely discloses her thoughts and feelings. These preferences are magnified as the couple manages the issues surrounding Kitty's infidelity: She wants to talk openly about it and he refuses. Only later in the film, when they are faced with challenges of life and death, does the couple find ways to confront the issues that have divided them. Again, it's easy to imagine how, if this film chronicled a lifelong marriage, we would see the same openness-privacy dialectic play out repeatedly.

SAY ANYTHING...

Film Data
Year: 1989
Director: Cameron Crowe
Length: 100 minutes
Rated: PG-13

Characters/Actors
Lloyd Dobler: John Cusack
Diane Court: Ione Skye
James Court: John Mahoney
Corey Flood: Lili Taylor
D.C.: Amy Brooks
Rebecca: Pamela Segall

Communication Course
Interpersonal Communication

Communication Concepts
Honesty/Lying
Relational Stages
Self-Disclosure

Pedagogical Perspective

This is a light romantic comedy with a serious message about the impact of dishonesty in primary interpersonal relationships. The movie could be used in high school or college classes (Diane and Lloyd's non-depicted sexual activity might be a sensitive issue for some audiences).

Synopsis

Say Anything... is a lighthearted tale about an unlikely couple. Lloyd Dobler (Cusack) is unsure what he will do after graduating from high school, except perhaps to pursue his dreams of becoming a professional kick-boxer. Diane Court (Skye) is valedictorian of her class and has plans for college—but unlike Lloyd, she has no social life. They attend a graduation party together, and Diane is pleasantly surprised at how comfortable and happy she feels around Lloyd. Their interest in each other grows and they date throughout the summer.

Diane's parents are divorced and she lives with her father (Mahoney), with whom she has always had open and honest communication. As Diane and Lloyd's relationship develops, Diane's relationship with her father begins to change. Diane's father believes Lloyd is complicating her life and he recommends that she break off her relationship with Lloyd before it becomes too serious. She acquiesces to her father's wishes. Neither Diane nor Lloyd is happy about the breakup, but she keeps telling herself it is for the best.

Diane and her father appear to have a healthy and positive relationship, but when she learns that he has engaged in illegal financial dealings involving the nursing home he runs, her trust in him is shattered. Diane realizes she wants and needs Lloyd and reaches out to him; he supports her while she deals with the devastating fact that her father is not the man she thought he was. Diane tries to reconstruct her relationship with her father before she and Lloyd fly off to England together.

Discussion Questions

1. What relational stages do Lloyd and Diane experience?

After admiring Diane from afar, Lloyd gradually works his way to and through the initiating stage. He begins with some indirect approaches, such as having lunch across from her at the mall (which she fails to notice). He then pursues a more direct approach and calls to ask her out. At first she turns him down, but Lloyd is persistent; she ultimately accepts an invitation to join him at a party.

On the way home from the party they engage in small talk, but they realize by the end of the date that they are interested in each other. During this experimenting stage, Lloyd has romantic interest in Diane. She feels a need to go slowly, defining their relationship as "just friends." During this stage, however, they tell each other about their feelings and fears. While their different backgrounds are the basis for a complementary relationship, they find they are also attracted to each other by their similarities (which are greater than they imagined) and their continued proximity to each other (Lloyd is her only friend and they spend a great deal of time together). By the time Lloyd teaches Diane how to drive a stick shift, it is clear that their relationship is becoming more romantic and that they are in the intensifying stage.

The move to the integrating stage is apparent when their relationship begins "going public." Lloyd meets Diane's friends at the nursing home and goes to a family dinner at her home, where he is perceived as Diane's boyfriend. Lloyd and Diane have a sexual encounter, which Diane recounts to her father and Lloyd discusses with his female friends. When Diane's father realizes she is in love, he expresses his fears to her. He is afraid that if Lloyd and Diane reach the bonding stage, it will distract her from the college plans that she and her father have made together.

Her father's pleas—and perhaps her own fears—launch Diane and Lloyd into new stages of relationship. Diane jumps quickly to the terminating stage, much to Lloyd's chagrin. He continues to call her and even stops by her house at night to blast "their song" at her window. Lloyd experiences the pain of rejection, while Diane feels guilty and misses Lloyd terribly. Their mutual grief suggests that their relationship had reached a high degree of intimacy. After Diane discovers that her father has been breaking the law, she reaches out to Lloyd. His love for her has not wavered and they appear to move to the bonding stage as they fly off to England together.

2. What were some of the reasons for self-disclosure between Diane and her father and between Lloyd and his female friends?

The openness between Diane and her father helps them maintain and enhance their relationship—a relationship that is very exclusive. In many ways, each is the other's best and only friend until Lloyd enters the picture. Diane even talks with her father about having sex with Lloyd. Her self-disclosure on this intimate subject seems prompted by a need for self-clarification, and perhaps by a desire for validation from her father.

Lloyd has three female friends who are his "sounding boards" throughout the movie. They know from the beginning about the crush that eventually turns into a love affair. He discloses many of his thoughts and feelings to them, looking for self-clarification and validation. Lloyd has a similarly open relationship with his sister, whom he calls from a phone booth in the rain to talk about his pain over the breakup with Diane. These examples reinforce research that shows that people prefer to self-disclose with members of the opposite sex.

3. Why did Diane's father choose to lie to her about his finances? What effect did his dishonesty have on Diane and their relationship?

Diane and her father have established what appears to be an open, honest relationship. On more than one occasion her father says, "You can say anything to me" (hence, the movie's title). Diane's perception of the relationship is evident when she tells her father, "It always feels good to tell you the truth, because if I can't share it with you, it's almost like it didn't happen." Unfortunately for Diane, her father's level of honesty is not the same as hers.

Mr. Court lies to Diane for several reasons. First, he lies to acquire resources that will benefit Diane. Second, he lies to keep her safe from legal repercussions. In other words, some of his reasons are other-oriented. At the same time, he also lies to save face and avoid conflict. He knows Diane would disdain his lack of financial ethics and his deceit in his dealings with her.

As it turns out, Diane confronts her father and he is forced to reveal that he has been lying to her. The result is traumatic for Diane because she believed their commitment to honesty was reciprocal. Diane begins to question everything she believed to be true. She wonders if her car and ring were bought out of love or as a scam for tax evasion.

When Diane becomes certain of her father's deceit, she unleashes her pain and anger on him: "You let me defend you, and you knew you were guilty and you let me become a part of it"; "I trusted you"; "I told you everything and you lied to me." Her father tries to justify his actions by pleading, "Do you think you know what this money is? It's not for me, this money is for you—for when you come back from England with honors. To set you up so you never have to depend on anybody again." Diane doesn't buy his reasoning; she sees the cover-up as a relational felony, not a misdemeanor. As a result, it drives her back to the person she now trusts most: Lloyd.

SHOPGIRL

Film Data
Year: 2005
Director: Anand Tucker
Length: 100 Minutes
Rated: R

Characters/Actors
Mirabelle: Claire Danes
Ray Porter: Steve Martin
Jeremy: Jason Schwartzman

Communication Courses
Communication Theory
Interpersonal Communication

Communication Concepts
Dimensions of Intimacy
Relational Dialectics
Stages of Relational Development
Uncertainty Reduction and Social Exchange Theories

Pedagogical Perspective

Younger viewers who are used to fast-paced action films may find this story moves too slowly for them. Nonetheless, it should be easy for most to appreciate Mirabelle's desire to find a satisfying relationship, and the challenges that search entails. The film is rated R for some sexual content & brief language. The film portrays a relationship in which a female character exchanges sexual favors for a comfortable lifestyle, but it hardly glorifies this sort of arrangement.

Synopsis

This bittersweet film follows the romantic adventures of twenty-something Mirabelle Butterfield (Danes). By day she sells gloves at Saks Fifth Avenue in Beverly Hills; by night she is an aspiring artist. In her search for love, Mirabelle meets two men who couldn't be more different. Jeremy (Schwartzman) is her contemporary. He is loveable, scruffy, funny, poor, and socially inept. Mirabelle's other romantic interest is Ray Porter (Martin), a suave millionaire who is old enough to be her father. Ray showers Mirabelle with gifts, and in short order they become lovers. From the beginning, Ray makes it clear that he is not interested in a long-term commitment, and Mirabelle agrees. But in time she realizes that this arrangement does not fulfill her emotional needs. By movie's end Mirabelle faces the dilemma of whether to continue in a comfortable but unfulfilling relationship with Ray, or to walk away and either choose Jeremy or risk being alone.

Discussion Questions

1. **Describe the relational stages in Mirabelle's relationships.**

During the initiating and experimenting stages of Mirabelle's relationships, we are able to witness several strategies of seeking similarities and reducing uncertainty. In his initial interaction with Mirabelle Jeremy chooses an abrupt "Hey, hi, hello" as a starting point. We can see Mirabelle's painful expression as she contemplates reciprocating Jeremy's advances. Only when they touch on their artistic similarity does the relationship have any hope of continuing. Ray chooses a more subtle, almost passive, strategy to gather information about Mirabelle. On their first date Ray even comments overtly on the sometimes awkward process of dating, at one point running out of questions to ask her. These scenes should provide several discussion points for students about initial interactions and beginning relational stages.

2. **Use Social Exchange theory to describe Mirabelle's relationship with Ray.**

In addition to uncertainty reduction, the film illustrates social exchange theory. Mirabelle processes the costs and rewards of deciding to continue dating either man. Though similar in age to Mirabelle, Jeremy's low self-monitoring, lack of finances, and general awkwardness are clearly costs. Still, there is something genuine about him. As for Ray, his charm, mysterious background, and wealth are certainly rewarding for Mirabelle. Mirabelle chooses Ray, only later realizing the implications of her choice.

3. **What dimensions of intimacy operate in Mirabelle and Ray's relationship?**

As Ray expresses in a voice-over near the end of the film, by keeping Mirabelle at a distance so as not to miss her when the relationship ended, this only intensified his loss when she did leave him. One lesson here is that relationships hold several dimensions of intimacy: physical, intellectual, and emotional. For some partners, one of these dimensions may be enough to sustain the relationship. For others, like Mirabelle, the absence of one dimension was reason enough to leave.

4. **What dialectical tensions operate in Mirabelle's relationship with Ray.**

As their relationship advances Mirabelle soon learns that while Ray can afford to shower her with gifts, he cannot give her what she truly needs: emotional intimacy. Ray's decision to hold Mirabelle close physically while at the same time keep his distance emotionally, is an example of the autonomy-connection dialectic. Sadly his "stay-away-close" management strategy backfires when he confesses to Mirabelle that he slept with another woman. This cost is too great for Mirabelle and she ends their relationship.

5. **What issues of honesty and clarity arise in the film?**

Ray tells Mirabelle that he likes seeing her but would like to "keep our options open," in other words he's not interested in a long-term commitment. He asks Mirabelle if she understands and she responds yes, but one has to wonder. In a subsequent scene, the movie shows how the same words are interpreted differently by each of them. Ray explains to a faceless therapist that he was completely straightforward with Mirabelle, that their relationship has no future. As Mirabelle talks about her date with Ray to her female coworkers, her perception is not the same as his: she believes Ray is going to cut down on his traveling, spend more time in LA, and ultimately spend more time with her. Their perceptions couldn't be more different. Whether Mirabelle talked herself into her own reality, or Ray told her what she wanted to hear, ambiguous language can create misunderstandings.

SPANGLISH

Film Data

Year: 2004
Director: James L. Brooks
Length: 131 Minutes
Rated: PG-13

Characters/Actors

John Clasky: Adam Sadler
Deborah Clasky: Téa Leoni
Flor Moreno: Paz Vega
Evelyn Wright: Cloris Leachman
Cristina Moreno: Shelbie Bruce
Bernie Clasky: Sarah Steele
Georgie Clasky: Ian Hyland

Communication Courses

Communication Theory
Intercultural Communication
Interpersonal Communication

Communication Concepts

Control and Power in Relationships
Defensive and Supportive Behaviors
Intercultural Communication
Relational Dialectics
Self-Concept and Identity Management

Pedagogical Perspective

   Spanglish should appeal to a variety of teaching perspectives, and to a variety of students: those whose families are dysfunctional, those whose first language is not English, and those who struggle to find their identity. The film also successfully contrasts two divergent styles of communication. On the one hand is Deborah Clasky, a thoughtless, selfish, and patronizing mother. On the other, there is her spouse John Clasky, a father whose first concern is rarely himself. When housekeeper Flor Moreno joins the family, she provides a healing presence for the family's wounds. The film is rated PG-13 for some sexual content and brief language.

Synopsis

   Spanglish opens with a scene at the Admissions office of Princeton University. In a voice-over, we learn that applicant Cristina Moreno identifies "the most influential person in her life" as her mother – Flor Moreno. What unfolds is a story about Flor's decision to work for an Anglo family, the Claskys, and how her choice changes their lives forever.

   The Clasky family consists of father John, mother Deborah, their two children Bernie and Georgie, and Deborah's mother Evelyn Wright. Flor quickly discovers that John is a highly successful, and perhaps overly-emotional, chef; Deborah is neurotic and hyper-competitive, lifting herself up by putting others down; Evelyn is an alcoholic, though kind and generous; and the children are desperate for the positive influence missing from their mother. When Flor and Cristina are forced to move in with the

Claskys during the summer, Flor loses all sense of privacy and is on the verge of quitting the job. By film's end, it's up to Flor to make decisions that at least provide a chance of the Claskys rebuilding their lives.

Discussion Questions

1. **Identify and contrast examples of Gibb's categories for defensive and supportive behaviors displayed by the characters. What effects do these behaviors have on their relationships?**

The film provides a number of defense-arousing and supportive behaviors for students to analyze. Starting with the defensive side, Deborah is the primary example of creating a negative communication climate. For instance, Deborah uses evaluative communication when she talks with her daughter Bernie about her weight and body image, sending powerful messages of disapproval. These feelings are compounded when Deborah purchases new clothes for Bernie that are intentionally too small, a questionable way to motivate her daughter to lose weight. Deborah is also judgmental of other characters' behavior, most notably her mother's alcoholism. In addition, Deborah is equally adept at exhibiting Gibbs' control and strategy behaviors. On several occasions she manipulates others to get what she wants: she forces Flor to choose between losing her job and moving in with the family, she secretly arranges a meeting between the principal of a private school and Cristina, and she boldly deceives Flor when she lies about Cristina spending the night at her house.

Contrary to Deborah's defense-arousing style, many of the other characters provide clear examples of supportive behaviors. For example, both John and Flor confirm Bernie's identity, with Flor going so far as to alter Bernie's new clothes so they fit and John frequently telling Bernie how "great" she is. When Flor comes to John desperate for advice about sending Cristina to a private school, John shows empathy when he confirms her feelings as normal. He also demonstrates provisionalism when he admits that he doesn't know what to do. This scene is also an excellent example of person-centered communication.

Through their supportive messages, it should be obvious to viewers that Bernie, John, and Flor have developed intimate, trusting relationships among each other. By contrast, Deborah's callous and calculating style of communication distances her from her family, ultimately leading her to find meaning and fulfillment elsewhere.

2. **Identify examples of one-up and one-down messages? Which relationships are complementary? Which are symmetrical?**

Several scenes in the film also illustrate dimensions of relational control and power, including complementary and symmetrical relationships. The relationships between Deborah and the other family members are clearly complementary, with Deborah frequently using one-up communication. For example, when she and John are arguing over how to discipline Georgie, Deborah insists on establishing a complementary relationship with the children; John is more willing to concede some control to Georgie, which infuriates Deborah. In the above-mentioned scene regarding Bernie's weight, Deborah once again uses one-up messages when she "encourages" Bernie to watch what she eats. Later in the film when Flor introduces Cristina to the Claskys, Deborah is so intent on controlling others that she has no qualms about "stealing" Cristina for shopping trips and sleepovers.

John, on the other hand, frequently utilizes one-down communication, almost to a fault. In fact, some of the film's more humorous moments are when John vents his frustrations about Deborah to others, because he cannot confront her directly. In addition, at his restaurant when a new employee bumps into John, he easily places himself in a one-down position by forgiving the employee. After John's four star review, his *sous-chef* requests, and receives, a twenty percent stake in the restaurant. When John informs

Deborah, she is outraged that she was not consulted on the decision. Indeed, John is so accustomed to being in a competitive relationship with Deborah that he is equally surprised when Flor gives in during a heated argument about paying Cristina for collecting sea glass. Taken as a whole, these scenes demonstrate how healthy relationships require flexibility and a balance of power, something unhealthy relationships typically lack.

3. **Which dialectical tensions do John and Flor experience, both with each other and independently? How do they choose to manage these tensions?**

The dialectical tension that John struggles to manage is the predictability-novelty of his business. Due to a four star review from a food critic, John progresses from an aspiring chef, to an extremely successful one. To manage this dialectic John first chooses denial. He tries to ignore the changes taking place, and instead works hard to "keep things the same." For example, after the review his restaurant is quickly booked-up for reservations months in advance, yet John wants to still allow for walk-in business; he cannot have both. John also worries out loud that too much success will change his employees for the worse, and change him. His next strategy for managing this tension is disorientation, and John quickly becomes overwhelmed with all the novelty and uncertainty his success has brought. In response, he locks himself in his cooler and binges on food, over-indulges in alcohol more frequently, and generally exhibits a state of depression. He ignores his developing marital problems and distances himself from Deborah.

Flor struggles with both the connection-autonomy and openness-privacy dialectics. When Flor begins working for the Claskys, she tells herself "this is only a job" and she fully intends to keep her working and private lives separate (a nod to segmentation). Still, she quickly finds herself growing attached to the children. When Flor discloses to Deborah that she has a daughter, something she has intentionally kept private, her wall of separation starts to crumble. It is noteworthy to point out that while every other member of the Clasky family both recognizes and respects Flor's private life, Deborah seems completely oblivious. Moving in with the Claskeys only intensifies Flor's struggle, since physical distance is no longer an option. Flor becomes so overwhelmed with the dialectical tensions and her loss of privacy, she chooses to quit working for the Claskeys and ends their relationship completely.

4. **How do the characters influence each other's self-concept? What influence does culture have on this process?**

The entire film is set up to demonstrate how Cristina's identity has been shaped by her mother, and how Flor has been "the most influential person in her life." As her significant other, Flor struggles throughout the film with questions that will impact Cristina's self-concept. Should she venture out and work for "Anglos," or stay in the comforts of her own Mexican culture? Does she allow Cristina to attend a private school, afraid that her daughter will forget her cultural heritage and instead become "like them?" Could she follow her heart and pursue a romantic relationship with John, knowing the devastating effect this would have on the children of both families? Each of these questions, and the decisions that Flor makes, show how mindful she is of her influence on Cristina and others. As Evelyn poignantly states, "You live your life for your daughter."

The other characters are not immune to influencing each other's self-concept. For instance, because of her mother's disconfirming messages regarding her appearance, Bernie not surprisingly engages in negative social comparison and self-fulfilling prophecy. Fortunately for her, John and Flor work hard to encourage Bernie to see herself positively.

Deborah's complex character provides the best example of self-concept and identity management. On the surface, Deborah presents a public self that is confident and assertive. Upon closer inspection, however, her private self is in conflict with her public image: Deborah does not know who she is, or at least she does not like who she has become. For example, when she is interviewing Flor for the housekeeper position, Deborah describes herself as the spouse of a top-chef which "makes me something," and off-handedly mentions that she used to be a designer but was let go, making her a "full-time mother, gulp." When she learns of John's four star review, instead of celebrating his achievement, she asks, "What about me, what am I going to do?" Deborah's perception of her self-concept displays how identity management is a collaborative process, performed in concert with others in her life.

UP IN THE AIR

Film Data
Year: 2009
Director: Jason Reitman
Length: 108 Minutes
Rated: R

Characters/Actors
Ryan Bingham: George Clooney
Alex Goran: Vera Farmiga
Natalie Keener: Anna Kendrick
Craig Gregory: Jason Bateman
Bob: J.K. Simmons
Jim Miller: Danny McBride

Communication Courses
Business Communication
Communication Theory
Interpersonal Communication

Communication Concepts
Computer-Mediated Communication
Perspective Taking and Person-Centered Messages
Relational Commitment/Dialectics

Pedagogical Perspective

Equally useful in courses on interpersonal communication and business communication, *Up in the Air* should prove to be a valuable teaching tool. The film contains clear examples of person-centered messages for interpersonal content, along with an almost sarcastic take on the use of computer-mediated communication in the business context. The film is rated R for some language and sexual content.

Synopsis

Ryan Bingham is an island surrounded by a sea of travelers. Working for a company that specializes in corporate downsizing, Ryan is paid, essentially, to fire people. And apparently he is very good at what he does: Ryan's company flies him around the country over 300 days out of the year. He also gives motivational speeches about "relational downsizing," and living one's life out of a backpack – a metaphor for Ryan's lifestyle. Clearly more at home on the road, Ryan's way of life is threatened when the company hires Natalie Keener, an overly ambitious college graduate who wants to revolutionize his business: Natalie believes firing employees can be done through teleconferencing and not in person. If that weren't threatening enough, Ryan begins a romantic relationship with fellow business traveler Alex, who causes him to question his self-imposed isolationism. Ryan Bingham might be an island, but he soon realizes that he is not alone.

Discussion Questions

1. **Compare and contrast Natalie, Alex, and Ryan, and their divergent views on relational commitment. How does each character define their romantic relationships? How do they manage the autonomy versus connection relational dialectic?**

Commitment is a conscious decision by partners to invest in their relationship. While sustained commitment can maintain a relationship through difficult moments, a lack of commitment often foretells the ending of a relationship. Likewise, how partners manage their relational dialectics can predict their success at keeping the relationship going. Arguably the primary dialectic that most relationships experience is the tension between autonomy and connection. The film offers three different viewpoints on how we define, maintain, and end our romantic relationships – call it a relational worldview.

Natalie's worldview is on the extreme connection side of the autonomy-connection dialectic. She literally defines her own identity by her romantic relationships. Natalie demonstrates her emphasis on connection when she tells Alex and Ryan that she followed her partner to Omaha (0:49:15), despite having a job offer in San Francisco. Idealistic to a fault, Natalie believes relationships should be like flow-charts: organized, scripted, and routine. Later when Ryan seems too casual with his relationship with Alex (1:00:43), Natalie berates him for his apparent lack of commitment. In Natalie's worldview, the tension between autonomy and connection is managed with selection, or nearly denying that autonomy exists.

Alex is the opposite of Natalie. For Alex, her worldview emphasizes extreme autonomy over connection. For example, Alex encourages Ryan (0:31:05) to think of their relationship as having no expectations or rules – Alex is completely non-committal. When Ryan asks her to accompany him to his sister's wedding (1:10:30), she agrees and Ryan is led to believe their relationship has moved to the next developmental stage. This belief turns out to be unfounded when Ryan discovers that Alex is married with children. Alex uses separation to manage the autonomy-connection dialectic, explaining (1:34:20) that her "real life" with her family is completely separate from her "escape" with Ryan. Students might find parallels between Alex's worldview and a 'friends-with-benefits' relationship, and what happens when one partner wants more commitment than the other.

At first Ryan's worldview seems more like Alex's. Ryan's motivational "backpack" speech (0:45:20) espouses a philosophy of non-commitment, and he believes relationships only "slow us down." For at least the first half of the film, like Alex, Ryan manages this dialectic with selection: he chooses autonomy over connection. However, Ryan's worldview begins to change (0:57:20) when realizes the importance of being committed to someone else, and even convinces his future brother-in-law that relationships are necessary (1:21:10). Although a painful lesson when he learns about Alex's family, Ryan manages to reframe his autonomy-connection dialectic.

2. **Analyze examples of person-centered messages Ryan creates as part of his job, and compare those with the messages he creates while not working. In which context is he more skilled at perspective taking? In which context is he more scripted?**

Perspective taking is one of three dimensions associated with empathy. To take the perspective of another involves understanding someone from their viewpoint – an appreciation of another's unique situation. A person-centered message, then, is the sender's attempt to tailor communication to match the other's uniqueness. A successful person-centered message comes across as genuine, sincere, and empathetic.

At work, Ryan is masterful at creating person-centered messages. Indeed, one reason for his continued success at firing people is his ability to adapt his communication to the specific context. Ryan is professional, with an air of caring. He is also a realist, without being condescending.

A prime example of Ryan's style is illustrated at the 0:32:15 mark in the film. Out on the road Ryan has been asked to "show the ropes" to Natalie, to demonstrate what he does. At this stage, however, she is there only to observe, not to say anything. After a string of emotional firings, an employee named Bob provides an especially challenging moment. Thinking she can assuage his anger, Natalie jumps into the conversation and offers several non-empathetic responses. Natalie's youth undermines her credibility and the results are not positive. Ryan steps in with what at first seems to be a non sequitur: he tells Bob that his kids never admired him. There is a method to his madness, however, as Ryan reminds Bob that his true passion is cooking. Bob's firing is not an ending, it is an opportunity to pursue his dream and gain his children's respect – a person-centered message.

Ryan's style at work is also an excellent example of the differences between empathy and sympathy, and the limits of each. Knowing that he cannot completely understand the emotions these fired employees are feeling, Ryan never commits the mistake of saying, "I know how you feel." He focuses his efforts on learning about each employee's background, but he does not allow himself to feel sorry for or sympathize with them. One could ask, then, is Ryan more emotionally intelligent than most people, or less?

Although he is skilled at perspective-taking at work, Ryan seems less adept within his personal relationships. At the 0:47:02 mark of the film, Natalie learns that her boyfriend has ended their romantic relationship. Shortly thereafter (0:48:20), in the middle of the hotel lobby, Natalie breaks down crying. Not having an empathetic script to fit this moment, Ryan does not know what to do. He seems embarrassed by the whole thing and suggests that they go up to their separate rooms to freshen up – not exactly a person-centered message. Fortunately for Natalie, Alex is there to offer some guidance and support.

Ryan does redeem himself, in his own way, when his sister's fiancé (Jim) gets cold feet on the day of their wedding (1:21:10). Again seemingly off in the wrong direction, Ryan agrees with Jim that marriage is difficult and "what is the point" anyway? However, Ryan corrects Jim's bearings by reminding him that the most important moments of his life were spent with someone else – and this time it appears that Ryan's perspective taking is truly genuine.

3. **Identify examples of computer-mediated communication (CMC) used throughout the film. In the business context, how effective is CMC? How do the characters use CMC outside of work?**

Media Richness Theory suggests that each communication medium (e.g., face-to-face, video chat, and text messaging) can be classified by the complexity of the message it can handle. The richest medium, because of its intricate mix of verbal and nonverbal cues, is face-to-face communication. Video chat (a form of CMC) still contains both verbal and nonverbal cue systems between senders and receivers, although persons are not physically present together, and is one step leaner than face-to-face. Since the message is only words on a screen (i.e., verbal cues), text messaging is the leanest of the three.

The film contains several, rather satirical, examples of the ubiquity of technology and CMC. For instance, after their first sexual encounter (0:15:40) Ryan and Alex immediately butt laptops to schedule their next tryst – without technology perhaps they would never see each other again. Later (0:38:20) when they both have trouble falling asleep, Alex and Ryan reach out through technology and engage in a little 'sexting' for comfort. Flirting, and relational stage advancement, no longer requires physical presence. Text messaging gets a bad rap (0:47:02) when Natalie's boyfriend uses the medium to break up with her. And later, Natalie quits her job through a text (1:39:30), prompting her boss (Craig) to complain that "nobody has any manners any more" – this being the same boss who wants to fire people through video chat.

The primary CMC storyline is Natalie's idea to revolutionize Ryan's business: she wants to fire employees through video chat. Ryan argues that the idea will never work, saying "there is a dignity" to his face-to-face methods – judging by examples in the film, he might be right. The first real test of Natalie's idea comes at the 1:03:30 mark of the film. However, Natalie soon learns that firing someone over a computer is not the same as in person. The weaknesses of the medium are revealed when Natalie is unable to adjust to the other person's emotional needs, and she has to yell to regain the employee's attention. In another scene (1:29:05), Natalie is training her staff with the new technology by role-playing and learning scripts. Ryan again balks at the practice, dismissing the technology as too impersonal and limiting. The irony here is that Ryan finds fault with firing people over video chat as being too impersonal and scripted, when in fact Ryan's talent is camouflaging his scripted communication as being truly genuine (see Question 2 above).

Although the film pokes fun at how CMC has become an unnoticed part of life, there is no debate that technology has changed the faces of business and interpersonal relationships. Asking students if these changes have made our lives better is a question worthy of discussion.

WAITRESS

Film Data
Year: 2007
Director: Adrienne Shelly
Length: 104 Minutes
Rating: PG-13

Characters/Actors
Jenna: Keri Russell
Earl: Jeremy Sisto
Dr. Pomatter: Nathan Fillion
Becky: Cheryl Hines
Dawn: Adrienne Shelly
Old Joe: Andy Griffith

Communication Courses
Communication Theory
Interpersonal Communication

Communication Concepts
Confirmation/Disconfirmation
Relational Stages
Social Exchange Theory

Pedagogical Perspective

Keri Russell is an actress students may recall from the TV show *Felicity*. And while some viewers may be tempted to dismiss the film as a just another "chick flick," many should be able to identify with Jenna's plight: feeling trapped in a relationship with seemingly no way out. Moreover, the film offers extensive illustrations of how costs and rewards influence our decisions to stay, or move on, in relationships – topics that students can likely relate. The film is rated PG-13 for some sexual content, language, and thematic issues.

Synopsis

Jenna (Russell) waits tables at a local diner somewhere in the American South, specializing in unique pies that she creates in her head. The pie names and ingredients typically reflect critical moments in Jenna's life, such as "Falling-in-Love Pie." Unfortunately, Jenna is also trapped in a marriage to a controlling and abusive husband named Earl (Sisto). Her plans to leave her husband are complicated when she learns she's pregnant with Earl's child, and when she begins an affair with the town doctor (Dr. Pomatter, played by Fillion). Through the process of composing letters to her unborn child, and through the support she receives from Dr. Pomatter and her coworkers, Jenna gains enough strength to break free of Earl and "start fresh."

Discussion Questions

1.   Provide examples of disconfirming messages Earl uses toward Jenna. How do these messages contribute to the climate of their marriage?

When viewers are introduced to Earl, they witness the climate of the marriage and learn why Jenna desires to leave him. On the one hand, Earl desperately seeks acknowledgement and endorsement from Jenna: He continually asks if she is listening to him and requests that she show interest in him. His stance might seem reasonable, if he wasn't so disconfirming to Jenna. Instead, marriage to Earl is a combination of control, superiority, and certainty. For example, one of Earl's favorite tactics is to command Jenna to repeat verbatim why he is right. In addition, any favors or requests made by Jenna are almost immediately denied by Earl, without discussion. And when he eventually learns that Jenna is pregnant, he forces her to promise that she will always love him more than the baby.

2.   Contrast Earl's disconfirming style with Dr. Pomatter's confirming messages.

Contrary to Earl's belittling and controlling communication toward Jenna, Dr. Pomatter provides the supportive relationship she needs. At perhaps her weakest moment in the film, Jenna is feeling overwhelmed with her pregnancy and on the verge of depression. Dr. Pomatter stops by to see her, and immediately recognizes her sadness. When Jenna exclaims that she "does not want to be saved," Dr. Pomatter replies, honestly, "I'm not here to save you." And instead of judging her or attempting to solve her problems, he holds her in his arms without saying a word. Later as Jenna teaches him to make a pie, she explains how awful she feels being pregnant. And once again instead of telling her how she should feel, Dr. Pomatter endorses her feelings as natural and normal. Yes, there are moments of kissing and touching that cannot be overlooked as physical components of relational intimacy. Still, as Jenna states, it was the conversation with Dr. Pomatter that propelled their relationship toward closeness.

3.   Use Social Exchange theory to explain Jenna's reasons for staying with Earl as long as she did, along with her ultimate decision to leave him.

Much of the film is devoted to Jenna's search for happiness, and most viewers would likely advise her to leave Earl immediately; the costs clearly outweigh the rewards. Yet, as predicted by Social Exchange theory the answer is not that simple. Living with Earl has lowered Jenna's comparison level for romance. For example, early in her relationship with Dr. Pomatter he compliments her appearance. She becomes flustered and uncomfortable because she's "not used to being noticed in that way." Jenna's comparison level of alternatives also influences the difficulty of leaving Earl. She wonders: Where would she go? How would she support herself and the baby? When Earl finds the money Jenna has been saving for her escape, all hope seems lost. Eventually, Jenna receives enough supportive communication from Dr. Pomatter that she begins to value her self-worth. She also obtains a large sum of money from Old Joe (Griffith) and achieves financial independence. Without either of these new elements, it's unlikely that Jenna would have found the courage to leave Earl.

4.   Describe how other characters in the film weigh the costs and rewards of their relationships.

Actually, much of the film can be used to demonstrate costs and rewards, beyond Jenna's relationships. For instance, in a very comical scene Dawn (one of Jenna's coworkers) tells Jenna about her recent dating disaster with "a mad stalking elf." And when Dawn confronts him, her criticism is so harsh that he is actually reduced to tears. Later, Dawn discloses to Jenna and Cheryl, another coworker, that she is now dating "the elf." When pressed to explain why, Dawn provides another example of comparison level of alternatives when she says, "Because nobody else wants me." Cheryl also has her own philosophy about finding relational happiness. In defense of having an affair with their boss, Cheryl explains how it's the excitement and anticipation that she finds rewarding, something that is missing from her own marriage.

5. Describe the relational stages of Jenna's relationship with Dr. Pomatter.

Waitress could also be used to illustrate stages of relational development, and specifically how some relationships do not develop sequentially. As Jenna puts it, her affair with Dr. Pomatter began as "just sex," a reference to Knapp's intensifying stage. Later, through intimate self-disclosure they reach the bonding stage, when Jenna calls Dr. Pomatter her "best friend" (and only the second best friend she has ever had, next to her mother). Perhaps because of the mutual trust and affection they have built, Dr. Pomatter is surprised when Jenna wants to completely end their relationship, not a gradual withdrawal but an absolute end. Her argument is a good example of how some relationships follow unpredictable paths, which could probably be said for *Waitress* as a whole.

WHEN HARRY MET SALLY...

Film Data
Year: 1989
Director: Rob Reiner
Length: 96 minutes
Rated: R

Characters/Actors
Harry Burns: Billy Crystal
Sally Albright: Meg Ryan
Marie: Carrie Fisher
Jess: Bruno Kirby

Communication Courses
Gender and Communication
Interpersonal Communication

Communication Concepts
Gender
Relational Stages

Pedagogical Perspective

This is a sweet, funny, and perceptive film that is well known to (and loved by) most college students. The now-famous "orgasm scene" and occasional rough language may make viewing uncomfortable for some, but most are familiar enough with the film that it doesn't faze them. This film is an ideal way to study relational stages. More information about gender issues in the film can be found in Em Griffin's textbook, *A First Look at Communication Theory. When Harry Met Sally...* is also a useful tool for discussing topics such as communication climate (which slowly changes from chilly to warm), conflict, and perception.

Synopsis

Harry Burns (Crystal) and Sally Albright (Ryan) are virtual strangers who get together for purely functional reasons: A cross-country car ride in which they share gas costs and driving. She quickly sizes him up as crude and insensitive; he appraises her as naive and obsessive. By the time they finish their journey, they are glad to part ways. However, they continue bumping into each other in the years that follow. Slowly but surely, a friendship develops between them—something that Harry declared could never happen because "men and women can't be friends; the sex thing always gets in the way." Harry and Sally try to set each other up with their friends Jess (Kirby) and Marie (Fisher), but Jess and Marie fall for each other instead. Harry and Sally try dating other people, but clearly they care deeply for each other. Ultimately, their friendship turns into love—but not without some sharp disagreements (and a short breakup) over the role that sex plays in male–female relationships. Their breakup ends when they realize how much they both like and love each other. They marry and (presumably) live happily ever after.

Discussion Questions

1. What gender differences are evident in Harry and Sally's communication?

In their conversations, Harry and Sally often exhibit communication patterns similar to those found in gender-related research. Harry tends to treat discussions as debates. He regularly tells jokes and enjoys having the first and last word. He rarely asks questions but is quick to answer them. For example, when Harry and Sally meet on an airplane, Harry (while talking about sex) says to Sally, "How long do you like to be held afterward? All night, right? See, that's the problem. Somewhere between thirty seconds and all night is your problem." Sally regularly asks questions of Harry but seems troubled by his competitive answers and approach to sex (Sally: "So you're saying that a man can be friends with a woman he finds unattractive?" Harry: "No, you pretty much want to nail them too").

Although Harry and Sally follow traditional gender roles in some of their communication, in other ways they do not. Harry is generally more willing than Sally to disclose his feelings, even with his buddy Jess (albeit his conversations with Jess usually occur while they are engaged in sporting activities, such as watching a football game or taking swings at a batting cage). Sally is more rational, practical, and circumspect than Harry. In an argument at Jess and Marie's house, Sally says, "Harry, you're going to have to try and find a way of not expressing every feeling that you have every moment that you have them." Harry counters by saying, "Nothing bothers you. You never get upset about anything." These breaks from traditional male/female stereotypes suggest that gender generalizations need to be handled with caution.

The story ends with a strong sense of hope for cross-gender communication. This is due in part to Harry's learning to "speak a different language." The argumentative style of his early interactions with Sally begins to soften when he expresses empathy (much to her surprise) in a chance bookstore meeting. Several times thereafter (e.g., in the park, at Jess and Marie's, on the phone after their breakup), he apologizes for his boorish behavior (something he never would have done on the trip from Chicago to New York). Near movie's end, Harry provides a warm and detailed description of why he enjoys being with and around Sally that includes the following: "I love that after I spend a day with you, I can still smell your perfume on my clothes. And I love that you're that last person I want to talk to before I go to sleep at night" (a far cry from his "How long do you like to be held?" argument on the airplane). Harry's growth as a communicator is a key to their relational development and success.

2. How does (or doesn't) Harry and Sally's relationship match Knapp's model of relational stages?

The stages of Knapp's relational model are illustrated well by Harry and Sally—but not in linear, sequential fashion. Harry and Sally go through the initiating stage at the beginning of the movie when introduced to each other by their mutual friend, Amanda. The car ride to New York is an extended exercise in experimenting, as they exchange and evaluate each other's ideas, opinions, and values. Their experimenting, however, ends in termination (as Sally laments, "Guess we can't be friends then . . . That's too bad, 'cause you were the only person I knew in New York"). As they part ways, they wistfully switch from shaking hands to hugging—a sign of the intensifying stage that never materialized.

At their next meeting (on an airplane), they again initiate and experiment—and again they terminate rather than intensify their relationship (with an emphatic "Goodbye, Harry" from Sally). Several years later, they initiate once more in a New York bookstore. This time, the experimenting that follows is more successful. Sally finds that Harry is a warmer, more empathic person than he used to be. As they walk through a park, he apologizes for his earlier conduct and they declare themselves friends—a sign that their relationship is finally intensifying.

Harry and Sally steadily move from intensifying to integrating (two stages that are sometimes hard to distinguish from one another). They talk on the phone at the end of each day; they eat and shop together; they discuss personal aspects of their lives; they joke with and tease each other. Their relationship appears to be escalating without abatement until they dance with each other on New Year's Eve—and suddenly they realize that they may be heading towards romance and bonding. They pull back and spend the next several scenes attempting to form romantic relationships with other people (differentiating). Differentiating can also be seen in their fight at Jess and Marie's house, as they argue about what sex means in a male–female relationship.

Harry and Sally ultimately have sex with each other and the relational roof caves in. Prior to their relationship with each other, sex has been a part of experimenting for Harry but a sign of bonding for Sally (Sally to Harry: "You want to act like what happened [sex] didn't mean anything." Harry to Sally: "I'm not saying it didn't mean anything. I'm saying why does it have to mean everything?"). Harry and Sally quickly experience circumscribing at dinner the following night ("It's so nice when you can sit with someone and not have to talk, huh?") and stagnating when they see each other at Jess and Marie's wedding. The pain of stagnating leads Sally to avoid Harry, as she refuses to answer his phone calls or attend a New Year's Eve party with him. Harry shows up at the party anyway and tells Sally all the reasons why they are integrated and ought to be bonded (see previous question). The relationship quickly moves from near-terminating to blissful bonding.

The moral of the story is that the stages in Knapp's model may be easy to spot in interpersonal relationships, but they don't always occur in neat, linear, sequential order.

SECTION IV
SAMPLE VIEWING GUIDES AND ASSIGNMENTS

Section I of this book describes a variety of ways and means for watching, analyzing, and processing feature films in communication courses. Turning those ideas into meaningful classroom activities can be assisted by providing students with viewing guides and assignments to ensure that they watch the films as communication case studies rather than as mere entertainment.

This section of the book offers examples of viewing guides and assignments for several different courses, from several different instructors. Some are simple and only ask the students to watch for particular concepts in the movies they view. Others are more complex, requiring significant analysis in conjunction with theories and readings—with the ultimate example being the *Babe* essay written by Stephanie Hamlett, an undergraduate student at Murray State University, who turned her assignment into a CSCA convention paper (p. 91).

Whether simple or complex, an instructor should provide some guidelines for viewing scenes and movies. Remember, many students will not be familiar with the concept of watching movies for analytical purposes; thus, they need some direction. At the very least, an instructor can cue students in advance that particular characters, scenes, and/or lines will offer illustrations of certain concepts and theories. On a more advanced level, the discussion questions in Sections II and III of this book can be asked of students before or after they watch designated scenes or films, then verbal and/or written responses can be assigned.

The following viewing guides and assignments are classroom "tried and true." Their variety should suggest that there are many methods and approaches for using feature films as instructional tools in communication courses.

VIEWING GUIDE: *BREAKING AWAY*

[Note: I use the following viewing guide in my interpersonal communication class in conjunction with our discussion of relationship development, deterioration, and dialectics. No writing assignment is given; I simply want the students to be prepared to discuss the movie, which we watch together in class at the end of the term.]

The following questions are designed to prepare you for our discussion of the movie *Breaking Away*. This is not an exhaustive list of questions; that is, we will probably address other issues besides the ones identified below. Nevertheless, they should provide you with a starting point for analyzing the story. Please use the back of this paper to jot down your observations of key moments and lines from the movie.

1. Who holds the power in this group of four guys at the beginning of the movie? On what basis is he given this power? What do the first few minutes of the movie tell us about the power structure of the group? How does this power structure change during the course of the story?

2. How does each of the four guys in this movie deal with the relational stage of differentiation? Which member seems most secure about "breaking away" from the rest of the guys? Who seems least secure? How do Mom and Dad Stoller cope with differentiation?

3. What dynamics of the dialectics of relationships can be seen in the movie?

Names of main characters:

Dave   Mom Stoller
Mike   Dad Stoller
Mooch   Katherine
Cyril   Rod

VIEWING GUIDE: *CHILDREN OF A LESSER GOD*

[Note: The following viewing guide was developed by Ron Adler for use in his interpersonal communication course.]

Be sure to view the film *Children of a Lesser God* by the deadline on the syllabus, either by renting it or by watching it in the Communication Lab. Along with viewing the film, be prepared to answer the following questions after completing each reading assignment in **Interplay**.

Chapter One
1. Use the transactional communication model to explain some of problems between James and Sarah.
2. To what degree was the conflict between James and Sarah related to <u>content</u> issues? (What were these issues?) To what degree did the conflict involve <u>relational</u> issues? (What were they?)
3. What dialectical tensions described in the text created challenges for James and Sarah?

Chapter Two
1. Based on information in the film, to what degree was the communication of characters affected by messages from significant others? (Identify those significant others and the messages they sent.)
2. What self-fulfilling prophecies might have accounted for the behavior of characters in the film?

Chapter Three
1. What perceptual factors described in Chapter 3 affected the relationship between James and Sarah?
2. How might James and Sarah use perception checking to resolve their conflict more constructively?
3. Apply the Pillow Method to analyze one specific conflict between James and Sarah.

Chapter Four
1. Identify which of the guidelines for emotional expression in Chapter 4 Sarah and James could have followed, and how doing so might have changed their relationship.
2. Which of the "fallacies" described in Chapter 4 did James subscribe to? Sarah? How might more rational thinking have changed their feelings and behavior?

Chapters Five and Six
1. What were the *linguistic* and *nonverbal* elements of <u>spoken language</u> in the film? What were the *linguistic* and *nonverbal* elements of <u>sign language</u>?

Chapter Seven
1. Which types of listening described in Chapter 7 were illustrated in the film? What were the consequences of these styles?

Chapter Eight
1. Which types of intimacy characterized the relationship between Sarah and James? Which types of intimacy <u>didn't</u> they achieve?
2. How well did the development of James and Sarah's relationship follow Knapp's model? (Pay attention to the text section on "Characteristics of Relational Development and Maintenance" as you answer this question.)

Chapter Nine
1. How closely did James and Sarah's relationship follow the characteristics of self-disclosure described in the first part of Chapter 9?
2. Which of the reasons for self-disclosure listed in Chapter 9 do you think explained James and Sarah's disclosures to one another?

3. Which of the "Guidelines for Self-Disclosure" in Chapter 9 did/didn't James and Sarah follow? How might their relationship have gone differently if they had followed all of the guidelines?

Chapter Ten
1. One element of conflict is perceived incompatible goals. Which of Sarah and James' individual goals were incompatible?
2. Which of the <u>personal</u> conflict styles in Chapter 10 did Sarah use? James? Which <u>relational</u> style did they use?
3. Describe how Sarah and James might have used the win-win approach described in Chapter 10.

DISCUSSION PREP FORM TEMPLATE:
ADVANCED INTERPERSONAL COMMUNICATION

[Note: I use the following prep form in my Advanced Interpersonal Communication course, a class in which ten movies serve as case studies for communication analysis. For each movie in the course, students must complete a prep form that analyzes the movie and ties in concepts from the day's reading (the readings are drawn from communication journals and books). When completed, these forms serve not only as the students' written assignments, but also as preparatory tools for the discussions held in class the following day.]

Discussion Question #1:

[Offer a question about the movie of the day that will provoke discussion in class]

Answer to Discussion Question #1:

[Supply an answer for Discussion Question #1. Your answer should be a minimum of 1-2 thorough paragraphs; more is encouraged. Your answer should demonstrate your analysis of the movie's characters, themes, symbolism, underlying issues, etc.—and more particularly, it should identify concepts and theories of communication illustrated in the film. You must incorporate information from the reader (including a direct quote or two from the reading for the day) in at least one of your Discussion Question answers.]

Discussion Question #2:

[Offer another question about the movie of the day that will provoke discussion in class]

Answer to Discussion Question #2:

[Supply an answer for Discussion Question #2. Your answer should be a minimum of 1-2 thorough paragraphs; more is encouraged. Your answer should demonstrate your analysis of the movie's characters, themes, symbolism, underlying issues, etc.—and more particularly, it should identify concepts and theories of communication illustrated in the film. You must incorporate information from the reader (including a direct quote or two from the reading for the day) in at least one of your Discussion Question answers.]

Key Line/Quote:

[Identify a key line/quote from the movie of the day]

Key Line Discussion:

[Discuss, in one paragraph, why you believe this was a key line/quote]

[Note: Your prep form should be typed, error-free, and at least two pages in length (longer is strongly encouraged)]

SMALL GROUP COMMUNICATION FEATURE FILM PROJECT

[Note: I use the following assignment in my small group communication class. It has proven very successful—and students report that they both enjoy it and learn from it.]

On [date], your project group will be responsible for 20-30 minutes of classroom instruction. Your assignment is to use a feature film to illustrate group communication concepts. Here are guidelines for preparation, presentation, and evaluation:

Preparation:

- Choose a movie. You may use any feature film except for *Dead Poets Society*, *12 Angry Men*, and *The Breakfast Club*.

- View the movie. Do this as a group at the time/location of your choice. Take notes, discuss concepts, and develop instructional strategies.

- Announce the movie. Tell the class as soon as you have made your selection. This announcement, which must be made in class no later than [date], will reserve the movie for your group (only one group per movie). No changes are allowed after this announcement.

Presentation:

- Describe the movie. Briefly provide the class with some basic plot/character descriptions to orient them to the film.

- Show clips from the movie. Carefully select and show a scene or scenes from the film that allows you to illustrate and discuss group communication concepts. A VCR/monitor and an overhead projector will be available in the classroom. All other arrangements (getting the video, taping/cueing the clips, etc.) are the responsibility of the presenting group.

- Analyze the movie. This is the crucial portion of your presentation and should involve the bulk of your time. I will leave this portion to your creativity and imagination. Lecture, discussion, skits, debates—the choice is yours, as long your focus is instruction about group communication. I expect you to weave in concepts/terms from the course, including information from at least one section of the textbook that we will not cover in class. Handouts and/or visual aids are strongly recommended. Decisions regarding "who does what" are up to your group. All members are not required to speak during the presentation; all are required, however, to contribute to the project.

Evaluation:

Your project will be evaluated by me and by your classmates (via confidential evaluation forms). While my assessment of your work will be the primary determinant of your project score, I will use your classmates' evaluations to assist my assessment. Your project score will be the grade that each member of your project group will receive as his/her Feature Film Project grade.

COMMUNITY AT WORK:
LEARNING ORGANIZATIONAL COMMUNICATION FROM *BABE*

Stephanie R. Hamlett

[Note: The following is an excerpt of an essay written by Stephanie Hamlett when she was an undergraduate student at Murray State University. She presented an extended version of this paper at the Central States Communication Association convention in April 2001 in Cincinnati. Ms. Hamlett would like to thank Dr. Michael Bokeno for his direction of this independent project. This essay is an example of how college students can and do make perceptive connections between communication theories and feature films.]

This essay will take a look at the movie *Babe*, whose central character is a talking pig, yet whose content provides for an exhaustive study of the basic theories of organizational communication. In this study, I use the film *Babe* to illustrate six theoretical approaches to organizational communication.

Synopsis of the Film

Throughout the film, Babe acts as the catalyst for radical changes that no organization initially wants to undergo; yet he is the promise of a future every organization wants to have. "This is a tale about an unprejudiced heart and how he changed our valley forever" (Noonan, 1995).

Babe begins his life in a large warehouse where pigs are bred for sale and butcher. Very soon after he is born he is given away to be a prize at the county fair where he is won by Arthur Hoggett. Farmer Hoggett is the owner of a farm whose lifeblood is sheep and their wool. The story line centers around the effect that the pig, Babe, has on the stable and orderly farm. Throughout the film, viewers follow Babe on his journey of self-discovery and watch as he changes life on the farm for everyone.

When Babe arrives on the farm, Fly, the mother sheepdog, takes him in until he gets on his feet. She acts as his mentor while he comes to understand the rules of life on the farm and how things work. He soon befriends a duck named Ferdinand who brings trouble with him. Already a nuisance in the eyes of Rex, the head sheepdog and 'boss' of the farm, he finds himself in a bind. On his path to discovering his niche, Babe comes upon the profession of sheep herding. When Mr. Hoggett gives him a chance to show his skills, he surprises everyone with his success. Rex, who feels he is being challenged and betrayed becomes enraged, fights with Fly, wounding her, and bites Mr. Hoggett. Shortly thereafter, he is sedated, leaving him incapable of doing his job. With the recent performance of Babe, Mr. Hoggett decides to put him to the test and enters him in the National Sheepdog Challenge. Although he is laughed at and ridiculed for this decision, he forges ahead. Babe, who has mastered his sheep herding ability through speaking to the sheep as equals, is startled to find that the sheep at the contest refuse to listen to a pig. With some unexpected cooperation between Rex and the Hoggett farm sheep, Babe is able to secure the password to speak to the sheep. In the end, he amazes everyone by winning the contest and wins the hearts of the viewers as well.

If organizational communication theories and principles haven't started jumping out at you yet, don't be concerned, they will soon overwhelm you. *Babe* illuminates Classical theory, Human Relations, Human Resources, Systems theory, Cultural theory and Critical theory, as well as organizational processes such as socialization and decision making, among others.

Approaches and Processes

If Weber, Taylor, and Fayol could have put their heads together with the purpose of creating a model organization to exemplify the combination of their beliefs about organizations, it would have looked much like that of Hoggett Farm. The ideas of these three men and those like them have been assimilated into what is known as the Classical Approaches. The three central ideas of the classical approach, specialization, standardization/replacability, and predictability (Miller, 1999), permeate every aspect of the organization. Every animal on Hoggett farm has its own task; chickens lay eggs, roosters crow at sunrise, cows provide milk, sheep provide wool, and dogs herd the sheep. No animal is expected to do more than what he/she is specifically there for.

Animals that fail to manage their own duties can be replaced quite easily and the routine order of a farm makes life usually quite predictable. Exceptions to the rule quickly surface in any organization though, and Hoggett farm is no different. It is home to an endearing duck named Ferdinand. While his role on the farm is quite defined, Ferdinand is not happy with his job of fattening up for Christmas dinner. He takes it upon himself to do the job of the rooster and crow in the mornings. His behavior is not tolerated by Mrs. Hoggett and he is quickly replaced by an alarm clock or, "mechanical rooster," if you will.

Functionally, the classical organization is a fine-tuned, well-oiled machine. In his Theory of Classical Management, Fayol highlights the importance of a strict hierarchy, division of labor, order, and organizational power. Surprisingly, Christmas dinner is not at the top of the Hoggett Farm organizational chart. Aside from the farmer and his wife, who will be discussed later in further detail, Rex, the head sheepdog, is the leader of the farm. It is widely known and accepted that his job is to keep the other animals in line. He is the driving authoritative force and center of command. Weber would classify his authority as traditional since the farm is in the middle of 'sheep dog country', and it is assumed that their position is one of great power and prestige. At his side, stands Fly, the mother figure of the farm. She is the female sheepdog who adopts Babe upon his arrival to the farm. Continuing down the hierarchy and cast of characters are Maa, the eldest member and leader of the group of sheep, Cat, the guardian of the household, Ferdinand the rooster-duck, a cow, and three entertaining mice. Interestingly enough, when Babe makes his appearance on the farm, he is the only one of his kind, a lone pig who knows less about how a pig should act than anyone.

Not only is the farm classical in its organizational structure but also in its relationships. Rex's beliefs and behaviors correspond closely to those of Taylor. His Scientific Management Theory details the main issues dealing with supervisor/subordinate relationships: there is one best way to do every job, workers must be properly selected according to criteria, and then properly trained, and there is an inherent difference between managers and workers (Miller, 1999). For Rex and Fly, the best and only way to herd sheep is through yelling and biting. As Fly explains to Babe, sheep are stupid and they only understand and behave when they are treated in this manner. Rex and Fly were both bred from national champion sheep dogs and they have been well-trained to perform their job. The inherent difference between them and the others is shown when the dogs are called to the house for supper one day. As Babe has been staying with Fly and her pups while he becomes accustomed to the farm, he follows the group as they head to the house. However, before he has a chance to go in, Fly stops him with the phrase, "only dogs and cats inside." When Babe questions this practice, he is met with the classical ideological response, "that's just the way things are."

Near the beginning of the film, at our first encounter with the mice, they sing a line that is fixed in the minds of the animals, especially Rex, "Pigs are definitely stupid." This mindset is obviously going to cause problems between the two and is the perfect introduction to how Human Relations Approach applies to Hoggett farm. Douglas McGregor (1960), in his Theory X and Theory Y, describes exactly the type of manager that Rex is. Each of the above theories is a description of a manager. The Theory X manager feels that his employees need to be carefully watched and controlled. They are not intended to have any control, this is the job of the manager. In addition, employees must be coerced into doing their jobs within the organization through schedules of reward and punishment. Theory X assumes that workers are inherently lazy, and incompetent. Rex personifies the theory X manager. He thinks that pigs are stupid, and that the sheep are stupid as well. At an animal meeting that is held after an unfortunate incident involving the cat, Rex declares to all of the animals that the farm turmoil is his fault because he was trying to loosen things up and no one was able to function without being told exactly what to do. Mrs. Hoggett could also be considered a Theory X manager. When she leaves town for a few days with some of the women from her community, she goes to extremes so that Mr. Hoggett will be completely taken care of. She gives explicit instructions on how to warm his dinner, which she had painstakingly pre-made, frozen, and labeled according to day. When she boards the bus she sighs and waves telling her friend she is not sure how he will make it through a day without her.

Mr. Hoggett, on the other hand has a more promising style of managing, that of the Theory Y manager. The Theory Y manager is characterized by thinking that employees enjoy their work and are self-driven to achieve goals of the organization (Miller, 1999). Mr. Hoggett is aware of the importance of satisfaction in a job well done to an employee, and realizes that employees possess a wealth of hidden potential. His first inkling of Babe's potential comes when he notices that Babe has separated the chickens into browns and whites. Later, in the field, Mr. Hoggett instructs Babe to drive the sheep from the shearing pen. Mr. Hoggett recognizes potential in Babe and gives him a chance to let his talents show.

One of the key differences in the Theory X and Y managers lies in what they believe to be the source of motivation of their employees. Theory X says it is just to survive, if they didn't have to work, they wouldn't. For the theory Y manager, motivation rests much deeper in intrinsic reward. These two extremes represent the top and bottom of hierarchy of needs described by Maslow. From the basic to the higher needs they are: physiological, safety, affiliation, esteem, and self-actualization. When Ferdinand "crows" in the morning, he is filling a need of safety (as he occupies a job that doesn't end in his consumption) and a need of self-actualization, he feels it is his calling to be the farm wake up call and he does his job with pride and dignity. When Babe is new to the farm and Ferdinand asks him to steal the alarm clock from the house, which necessitates the breaking of the rule against pigs in the house, his need for belonging prevails over the threat of punishment. In yet another example, Mr. Hoggett shows how important the higher level needs are when he uses the idea of having 'next years prize winning pig at the fair' as a motivator for Mrs. Hoggett to not have the pig for Christmas dinner as she had planned. With the thought of her future achievements in her head, she quickly changes her tune.

Seeing as how Babe, the pig, has been virtually raised by Fly, the sheepdog, it is natural that he feels somewhat dog-like. Perhaps this is what led to his fascination with the sheep. Much like a child admires the profession of his parents, Babe admired the work of the sheep dogs, and thought that it would be a suitable position for him on the farm since he hadn't found one quite yet. In his quest to achieve this success, Babe has one major hurdle to jump; he is a pig, not a dog. On a whim of Farmer Hoggett, Babe is given a chance to herd the sheep. To help him in his first attempt, Fly gives him a little advice. She tells him that it is all in the attitude, he must show the sheep who the boss is. As Babe soon finds out, neither his bark nor his bite are going to get him anywhere. Then he tries a new approach, and talks to the sheep, nicely. They explain to him that given the proper respect, they are perfectly intelligent enough and willing to obey. Babe is overwhelmed by this new idea, and so are Rex, Fly, and Mr. Hoggett when they see the sheep walking into the field two by two. When asked how he accomplished this feat, he simply replied, "I just asked them."

Babe's new knowledge gives him the qualities of a team manager. High concern for people as well as high concern for production, as described by Blake and Mouton, founding theorists of the Human Resources approach, characterize this type of management employed by Babe. It allows the goals of both parties to be met through working together to maximize production, and is viewed as ideal. Babe returns to Fly full of new ideas and ready to share them, however, management is not willing to listen. Rex, the classical manager feels as though the chain of command has been breached and that Babe and Fly have overstepped their boundaries. Although it is very apparent to Fly, Babe does not understand what he has done wrong. In his eyes, the animals on the farm should work together and share information. He is confused at why Rex does not feel the same way.

Possibly one of the most difficult theories to grasp in the study of organizational communication is systems theory, and this is one of the areas in which *Babe* will truly shine as a teaching tool. Byers, (1997) says that "while classical theorists perceived of the organization as a machine-like process that operated through control, systems theorists perceived that organizations are more like living organisms with their own life cycle" (p.27-28). A farm, a true example of a living organization, is the perfect setting to describe and understand this theory. Systems theory has several features that construct its nature. The basis of these is the idea of hierarchical ordering. This simply stated means that each organization is made up of different levels of systems. Each system has its own set of sub-systems and is, itself, a sub-system to yet a larger system. Each of these systems are interdependent, and they are open systems, ones permeable to outside information. On Hoggett Farm, there are countless examples of this hierarchy and interdependence. The farm can easily be divided into two parts: the house and the barn. While they are two separate entities, they cannot function without one another. Without the animals, the farm would fail. The same is true in reverse; without the Hoggetts, there would be no animals. There is an inherent need for "working together" and "reliance" that was not given consideration in the previous approaches. This idea of working together gives way to the idea of wholeness, or holism. Holism reflects the notion that the total, or end result, is greater than the sum of its parts. Sometimes referred to as synergy, holism stresses the importance of interdependence. Babe is very aware of this concept and does his best to introduce it to the others but unfortunately he is usually met in opposition. In his mind he has discovered a better way to herd sheep through politeness and caring, so as a part of an interdependent system, he feels it is crucial to pass this information on. He knows that by working together with the sheep, they will be more effective in herding than if he withholds the information. Systems theory relies on this process of input and output; it also stresses the importance of 'thruput', the process by which the new information is processed and internalized.

One of the major systems theories is the Cybernetic system. This system is broken down into four main components: Goal, Mechanisms, Behavior (target), and Feedback. An excellent example of how the cybernetics theory plays out can surprisingly be seen in something mechanical. In the beginning of the film Mr. Hoggett begins work on his gate. His goal is to fix the gate so that it will open, close, and latch by pulling a chain. With this goal in mind, he creates a machine he hopes will achieve his goal, (the mechanism). Although the machine works, the gate closes and latches very heavily and loudly, (the behavior). The feedback sent to Mr. Hoggett reflects the behavior of his invention, and upon comparison, they are not in congruence. The violent closing of the gate is not what Mr. Hoggett envisioned as his goal. When incongruence is found, new mechanisms to achieve the goal are looked for. In the case of the gate, the machine used to control the gate was adjusted until the gate shut with ease and silence.

The ideas constructed by the Cybernetics Systems theory are very important. However, there are underlying inferences that need to be clarified. Most importantly is the idea of equifinality. The principle of equifinality states that several different mechanisms can be used to reach the same system goal. Mr. Hoggett can employ either the dogs or the pig to herd the sheep. The two methods are drastically different, yet the goal is still accomplished. This idea is crucial to the survival of an organization. Since we have determined that organizations are open systems and that they are permeable to the environment, we can conclude that as the environment surrounding the organization changes, so will the mechanisms.

Hoggett Farm is itself a system operating in the larger system of the world. The technological advancement of the globe permeates the operation of the farm. At first, the Hoggetts are reluctant to use the fax machine given to them as a Christmas gift from their children. Yet as time progresses, Mr. Hoggett decides to use the machine to send in Babe's application to compete in the National Sheepdog Trials. This embracing of new mechanisms will help the farm avoid the trap of negative entropy. This phenomenon is described by Miller as the "tendency of closed systems to run down" (1999, p.74). Being open to information from the environment will allow the organization to not only avoid closing itself off, but will allow it to grow and expand.

Another important step in the Cybernetics theory deals with feedback, or more accurately, the reaction to feedback. Feedback, like entropy can be considered either positive or negative. Negative, corrective, or deviation-reducing feedback describes situations in which deviations from the standard, or conventional mechanisms are seen as disruptions of the process. While this type of feedback is typical in most organizations, it can stifle creativity and growth within an organization. Ferdinand, the "rooster-duck", is met with this type of feedback in response to his crowing. Since the crow of a duck is a deviation of the standard rooster crow, it is looked upon as a nuisance, while in fact, it still gets the job done, and provides an employee of the organization with a sense of pride and belonging. Positive feedback, which is also referred to as growth or deviation-amplifying feedback works in just the opposite way. Divergence from the norm is considered good for the health of the organization. When the idea of a pig that herds sheep presents itself, it is met by positive feedback from Mr. Hoggett and he is rewarded when Babe is successful at herding. However, if Mr. Hoggett would have been unaccepting, as was the rest of the world, he never would have won the competition, and the world might never have been made aware of the possibilities of pigs as sheepherders. Without Babe and Mr. Hoggett's mindsets, the farm would have definitely continued on a downward spiral. Luckily they grasped the importance of growth and change that remains such an enigma to classical organizations, and to the other members of the farm.

Cultural approaches to organizational communication help to uncover the fundamental values that prompt each organization to operate in the manner it does. While organizational culture is not something that is written procedure or taught in orientation, it plays a crucial role in the operation of the organization. When there is something or someone who does not fit with the culture, it causes distress within the organization. This is pointed out in the previous example of Babe and Mr. Hoggett bringing about change. The reason these ideas are viewed negatively by the organization is because change is not something that the overall culture of the farm values. Regardless of which view of culture one takes of an organization, there are countless examples present in the Hoggett Farm.

In Corporate Cultures, Deal and Kennedy (1982, p.4) say, "whether weak or strong, culture has a powerful influence throughout an organization; it affects practically everything—from who gets promoted and what decisions are made, to how employees dress and what sports they play." In his model of culture, Edgar Schein proposes that culture exists on three different levels within an organization. These levels are artifacts and creations, values, and basic assumptions. Artifacts and creations include dress, technology, network configuration, architecture, and communication during meetings. Artifacts on Hoggett farm would include the use of a new gate, the fax machine, how orders are passed down (i.e. from Mr. Hoggett, to Rex, to the rest of the animals), where the animals are allowed (i.e. no pigs in the house), and Rex's formal and authoritative delivery at meetings. While these artifacts are visible to outsiders, it is hard to understand the meaning behind them. For example, there is no written reason why pigs aren't allowed into the house. As far as an outsider is concerned it could be because Mrs. Hoggett is allergic to pigs. The second level of Schein's model is values. These values represent the ideas behind the behavior of members in the organization. At one point in the movie, Mr. Hoggett is ready to shoot Babe for killing a sheep, because of his value that no animal should harm another. He further supports this value when he sedates his prize-winning sheepdog Rex for injuring Fly. Behaviors that support values, such as these, strengthen the culture. However, many times in organizations, behaviors are not representative of what the values state, necessitating further questioning of what the basic assumptions are. These basic assumptions, Schein's third level, are so engrained into the minds of the members of the organization that they are never questioned and are taken for granted by everyone. This makes them difficult to uncover and even more difficult to explain.

The nature of all culture is very complex and it is also sensitive. When a newcomer is being socialized into an organization's culture, it is very important that the individual come to understand the culture or they will have severe problems finding their role in the organization. Babe's quest to discover the culture of the Hoggett farm gives us incredible insight into what potential a culture has in shaping a newcomer. When Babe tries to enter the house for the first time and is forbidden, he questions why and is met with Fly's equivalent of "just because." Babe is now required to interpret this message on his own and since he is given no further explanation, it is likely that he will conclude that he, in his role as a pig, is not worthy of the house. It is in this manner that employees will discover the basic assumptions of the organization. Having figured this out, Babe is in the position to either accept these assumptions, thereby perpetuating them, or challenge the assumptions, which is what Babe does. While "values tend to be relatively stable and enduring" (Robbins, 2001, p.62), cultures are not stagnant and they can be changed on the organizational level as *Babe* proves.

In the end of the film, the culture of the farm has become an excellent example of Deal and Kennedy's strong culture. It has adopted *values* of change and innovation, and encouragement. The farm possesses a *hero*, one who exemplifies these values, in the person of Mr. Hoggett. Babe is rewarded through *rites and rituals* when he is allowed to come inside and sleep when he successfully performs outside of his prescribed role. Lastly, a *cultural network* is established when Babe competes with Mr. Hoggett in the National Competition. There, others are allowed to see that innovation is something valued in the Hoggett organization. These cultural approaches are unique in the fact that they operate alongside each of the other theories. While a systems theorist and a traditional theorist may operate on different premises, cultural theories still apply to each equally.

The last of the major approaches to studying organizational communication, and another one of the most difficult for students to grasp is the critical approach. Unlike the five approaches discussed thus far, the critical approach is not a mechanism to "understand or explain organizational communication phenomenon" (Miller, 1999, p.13). The purpose of critical theory is to raise awareness of the constraints that the organization places on its members and to facilitate the members to work free from these constraints and force change in the organization. Particularly, critical approaches regard organizations as "instruments of oppression" (Daniels, Spiker, & Papa, 1997, p.12), or "sites of domination" (Miller, 1999, p.113). While this instantly stirs up negative connotations in most minds, *Babe* helps students to understand that even though critical theory deals with many negative issues, it is not proposing that all organizations are controlling, manipulative powerhouses, designed to break down creative, free-thinking employees. On the other hand, it strives to uncover the subconscious nature of these phenomena. As with the other approaches, different views vary slightly in their details. However, there are central themes important to all critical theorists. Most importantly is the function of power within an organization, and the legitimization of that power (Daniels, Spiker, & Papa, 1997). This is not simply the traditional power that is granted by position, but the power that exists within the communication relationship, and the false justification of that power. Embedded in these communication relationships are the ideas of hegemony and ideology. Hegemony "refers to a process in which a dominant group leads another group to accept subordination as the norm" (Miller, 1999, p.119). Through different processes, these ideas of subordination are embedded into the psyches of the employees until they no longer question the authority at all. If asked about the source of the authority, they would probably not be able to give an answer other than, "that's just the way things are", a popular aphorism in *Babe*. Hegemony is made possible through the formation of ideologies, which are our personal sets of taken-for-granted assumptions through which we analyze and perceive our worlds.

As most students at this level, I would assume, are not familiar with Marxist thinking and the historical roots of these ideas, example and simulation are key for explaining these theories, possibly more so than for any of the others. In the film, Babe can actually be looked at as playing the role of a critical theorist on the Hoggett farm. As he has not been indoctrinated by the same ideology and been subjected to the same hegemony as the rest of the organization, the power structure is more apparent. Viewers have the privilege of being directly presented with the ideology of the farm by the mice. "Pigs are definitely stupid…Pork is a nice sweet meat…A pig that thinks it's a dog, Ha," these statements are all examples of the ideology that Babe is trying to uncover. They shape the way that everyone perceives pigs. Babe's accident in the house is not surprising to the farm because pigs are stupid; Babe should not try as hard to find a job on the farm because his only true purpose is to be Christmas dinner; and Babe should definitely not herd sheep, because that is only for dogs.

When Babe first joins the farm he is a quiet observer of the culture of the farm. Yet, he soon begins to question behavior. After receiving conflicting messages from the sheep and the dogs about each other, he decides that he will not rely on the perceptions of others to form his own. Throughout the film, Babe continues on this process of discovery. He becomes aware that for some reason, dogs feel as though they have to be hateful to the sheep, animals and humans must conform to certain roles, and that there are unquestionable sources of power on the farm. Babe does his best to understand, in his naïve and sweet manner, why things are as they are. He discovers, for example that both Rex and Fly are from a long line of national sheepdog champions, and that for them, failing in their job, makes life not worth living. This underlying ideology influences every action that Rex makes. He, of course, was not the one who came up with the idea of subordination and control as the only way to get the job done; it is just too inherent for him to see otherwise.

Babe is also presented with mixed issues of gender and control that he has to interpret. While Rex and Mr. Hoggett both run their respective parts of the organization, the film presents them each with female counterparts that contend for control. It is interesting how these relationships play out in the organization. Both Mrs. Hoggett and Fly command respect and display authority to their counterparts, however, when they become too involved and overstep certain invisible boundaries, their power is rebuked by the male in the situation. It is almost as if they are allowed to perceive themselves as having a certain amount of authority and control, yet in reality, it is only permitted when the decisions they make do not lessen the authority of their counterparts. For example, Rex is not happy when he finds that Fly has allowed Babe to stay in the barn until he gets his bearings. Fly still remains strong in her decision and Rex backs down. However, after she has spent the day helping Babe learn to herd sheep, Rex fights with her, and injures her leg. Likewise, Mrs. Hoggett lives under the belief that she single-handedly rules the house. In actuality, she is merely fulfilling the wishes of her husband. When she begins measuring Babe to see if he will be big enough for the Christmas meal, Mr. Hoggett shows his control over her by convincing her of how nice she would look next year as the owner of the prize winning pig at the state fair. Through this mechanism he asserts his control so that she makes the decision he wants, yet he allows her to feel she is still in perfect control. This is yet another excellent example of hegemony in the Hoggett organization. Although it may seem contradictory to pin something so negative to a hero of the organization, it helps teach students that even the most ideal members of the organization can fall victim to supporting these behaviors.

In his attempt to understand organizational life, Babe is always questioning the strength and validity of these encounters. Emancipation, Babe's goal in his questioning, most relates him to the critical theorists. Emancipation occurs when these power structures have been dismantled so that employees are able to consider alternatives to the traditional processes of the organization thereby increasing their own possibilities for self-actualization in the workplace. Ideological hegemony is a formidable opponent, yet because it is such a latent and concrete aspect of the organization, its deconstruction can be seen as radical and disruptive. It is for this reason that the role of the critical theorist is so important in organizational life. This approach fosters thinking, analysis, and change, three items necessary to the life and growth of an organization.

Conclusion

The lighthearted story and deep message of *Babe* make it a perfect film for use in the classroom. Students are likely to enjoy the assignment, as it will probably be quite out of the ordinary and a nice change of pace. Its direct relation to subject matter is an exceptional advantage and will hopefully provide for varied student response. There are countless examples to build from in constructing their analyses. Thus, each student is likely to see something everyone else misses. They may just be animals, but they have a lot to teach us.

SECTION V
ADDITIONAL FILMS WITH MINI-VIEWING GUIDES

The following films are some additional contemporary films that can be used to illustrate communication concepts. Each of the film entries in this section provides the following information:

Film Data: Year, Director, Rating
Communication Concepts: Primary communication topics in the film (listed alphabetically)

AMERICAN SPLENDOR

Year: 2003
Directors: Shari Springer Berman, Robert Pulcini
Rating: R

Communication Concepts
Communication Climate (Transactional Communication)
Communication Competence
Relational Intimacy

American Splendor is a story within a story within a story. It is based on the real-life adventures of Harvey Pekar, a grumpy and pessimistic file clerk who writes autobiographical comic books. The real Harvey Pekar offers narration for the movie, but his character is played in the film by actor Paul Giamatti. To make things even more surreal, the film shows the real Harvey talking about the character Harvey as he writes about the cartoon Harvey.

Harvey lives a sad and lonely existence until the equally odd and neurotic Joyce Brabner (played by Hope Davis) drops into his life. Joyce is immediately attracted to Harvey, and in very short order they become husband and wife. Over time, Harvey becomes a successful comic book writer, he fights and defeats cancer with Joyce's loving support, and the couple adopts a young girl.

As a communicator, Harvey does just about everything wrong. He isn't skilled at maintaining intimate relationships, in part because he is incessantly pessimistic and gloomy. He and Joyce impulsively decide to get married on their first date, moving from (in Knapp's terms) experimenting to bonding in a matter of minutes. By almost any measure of communication competence, Harvey doesn't score well. He doesn't have a wide range of behaviors, he's not skillful at choosing appropriate responses, and he blurts out inappropriate comments with little or no self-monitoring.

Despite all these shortcomings, Harvey and Joyce ultimately create a relationship that works well for them. One reason for this success is their level of personal and relational commitment. Harvey recognizes his need for intimacy and commits himself to escaping his loneliness, despite his pessimism and previous relational failures. Joyce remains committed to Harvey, quite literally "in sickness and in health." They each learn to accept the other's shortcomings, focusing instead on their personal and relational strengths.

Harvey and Joyce aren't ideal communicators according to textbook criteria, but together they illustrate the transactional nature of communication. If there is a moral to their real-life story, it's that less-than-perfect people can form loving and meaningful relationships, even if they don't follow all the "rules" of communication competence. That's because communication is a unique, relational process between individuals who create their own culture—and for Harvey and Joyce, their relational whole is much greater than the sum of its parts.

A BEAUTIFUL MIND

Year: 2001
Director: Ron Howard
Rating: PG-13

Communication Concepts
Communication Competence
Perception

John Nash (Russell Crowe) is a brilliant mathematician whose interpersonal skills are virtually nil. He generally avoids interaction with others; when he does talk, he offends people with his bluntness and insensitivity. Many of his blunders aren't intentional—he's simply an odd duck who is more comfortable with numbers and theories than with people and relationships.

In one example of communicative incompetence, Nash approaches a pretty young lady at a bar. He hasn't a clue how to start a conversation, so she has to prod him to buy her a drink. He then suggests (in "scientific" terms) that they should cut past the small talk and move quickly to intercourse (which he describes as an "exchange of bodily fluids"). She slaps him, calls him a name, and walks out.

Ironically, Nash takes a similar approach with Alicia (Jennifer Connelly), a student who has a crush on him (the feeling appears to be mutual). When he frankly explains that he's hoping their relationship will soon culminate in sex, she interprets his comments as a clumsy but well-meaning statement of love and she kisses him passionately. The scene illustrates the transactional nature of communication competence. Although John's comments are awkward and inappropriate, Alicia sees through to his innocent intent and creates a romantic moment.

Alicia's ability and willingness to perceive John positively is crucial to their relational success. For instance, John's marriage proposal to Alicia is anything but romantic—he arrives late to dinner, gives her a stone rather than a ring, and mumbles a few words about his lack of faith in long-term commitments. Alicia is indignant at first, but then she says, "Give me a moment to redefine my girlish notions of romance." Once she reframes the situation, she makes up for his incompetence with her own competence—and eventually agrees to marry him.

Later in the story, after John has fallen victim to schizophrenia and delusions, a friend of the family asks how Alicia is holding up under the strain of "losing" her husband. She responds by explaining how she remembers John at his best and clings to those memories, despite the present reality. The scene illustrates the notion of "positive distortion," in which married couples see only the best in each other and choose not to focus on negative characteristics.

For the record, *A Beautiful Mind* takes some liberties with the real-life story of John Nash and his wife Alicia—but many of the movie's moments are accurate. Regardless of whether the story is fact or fiction, it illustrates well the transactional nature of communication competence.

BEND IT LIKE BECKHAM

Year: 2002
Director: Gurinder Chadha
Rating: PG-13

Communication Concepts
Culture
Honesty/Ethics
Relational Dialectics
Self-Disclosure

Jesminder "Jess" Bhamra (Parminder Nagra) is a young lady who is caught in the middle of conflicting goals, relationships, and cultures. Her parents want her to embrace her Indian heritage and traditional Sikh upbringing, but she would rather play soccer in the parks of London. When she's invited by new friend Juliette (Keira Knightley) to try out for a local soccer team, Jess knows her parents would never allow her to participate—so she doesn't tell them. She makes the team and attends their practices and games in secret.

Secrets are a central theme of this movie, as several characters wrestle with the dialectical tension of openness versus closedness. They choose not to self-disclose important information for a variety of reasons, ranging from saving face to saving relationships. Throughout the story, discovered secrets often lead to hurt and a sense of betrayal—yet it's easy to see that most of the secrets were being kept for good reasons.

The title of the film is a reference to the kicking style of soccer star David Beckham, whom Jess idolizes. It is also a metaphor for the characters' relational communication. While Jess sometimes bends the truth, she is also trying to get her parents to bend their ways (similar to a process that Juliette is going through with her mother). The key to maintaining these and other relationships in the movie is learning how to "bend without breaking."

Ultimately, Jess decides to openly pursue her goals and dreams, even if it disappoints the people she loves. In all of her relationships—with family, friends, and lovers—Jess finds that she must balance connection with autonomy, predictability with novelty, and closedness with openness. By movie's end, she appears to be up to the challenge.

BREAKING AWAY

Year: 1979
Director: Peter Yates
Rating: PG

Communication Concepts
Leadership
Power
Relational Dialectics
Relational Stages
Self-Concept/Identity Management

Breaking Away is a coming-of-age film about four high school graduates from Bloomington, Indiana who are trying to figure out what to do with the rest of their lives. The young men are referred to disdainfully as "Townies" and "Cutters" by the college students at Indiana University ("Cutters" is a reference to their fathers' occupation as stone cutters in the local quarries). The group is led by Mike (Quaid), a former high school quarterback who is also the group's quarterback. Dave (Christopher) dreams of being Italian, adopting their language and bike racing as a way of escaping his lot as a Cutter. Cyril (Stern) is witty but gangly and Moocher (Haley) is shrewd but short. These odd bedfellows have agreed, according to Cyril, "to waste the rest of their lives together."

The movie is indeed about "breaking away." Dave, Moocher, and Cyril pursue jobs, girlfriends, and entrance to college—all of which threaten to break them away from the group that Mike leads with an iron fist. Dave also tries to break away from being a Cutter by pretending to be an Italian exchange student, a ruse that helps him charm an IU co-ed (Douglass). His fantasy breaks down, however, when the Italian bike team he reveres cheats its way to victory at Dave's expense. After a heart-to-heart talk with his father (Dooley), Dave decides it is okay just to be Dave Stoller—and to go to college. His new sense of identity helps him supplant Mike as leader of the group, as he leads the Cutters to win the Little 500 bike race against the college students. The four young men, as well as Dave's parents, learn to take pride in their heritage while moving forward toward their personal goals.

This is an ideal film for undergraduate classes. Its coming-of age themes resonate with those who are trying to decide what to do about their high school friendships, relationships with their parents, and life goals. The movie's only limitations are its age (the 1979 fashions and hairstyles are dated, but the issues in the story are timeless) and its focus on male interaction. One way to address the latter issue is to compare and contrast the movie with a film that focuses on female interaction, such as *Steel Magnolias*.

A Viewing Guide for this film is available on p. 106.

CATCH ME IF YOU CAN

Year: 2002
Director: Steven Spielberg
Rating: PG-13

Communication Concepts
Deception
Honesty/Ethics
Persuasion (Compliance Gaining)
Self-Concept/Identity Management
Self-Disclosure

Frank Abagnale (Leonardo DiCaprio) is a teenager in a family that is slowly falling apart. His father is deep in debt, his mother is having an affair, and Frank is trying to find an identity. In the footsteps of his father (who cons his way into and out of situations), Frank learns that with a little ingenuity and a lot of chutzpah he is able to impersonate a teacher, a pilot, a doctor, and a lawyer. These false fronts allow him to become rich, admired, and respected—and lonely.

To accomplish his goals, Frank uses a variety of compliance-gaining tactics. A primary tool is rewards: He compliments people (particularly women), gives them gifts, and treats them with a level of respect they don't normally receive. In return, they are more than willing to provide information and resources that Frank needs to pull off his impersonations. Another tactic he uses is direct requests. He brazenly asks for—and gets—a variety of favors and special treatment. These requests are successful in part because Frank, while young, presents himself as a high-credibility source. He wears uniforms, speaks with confidence, and rarely looks flustered—even when he's shaking inside.

Although identity/impression management is a feature of competent communication, Frank crosses the line from other-oriented appropriateness to self-serving deceit. The more faces and fronts he constructs, the more he loses his sense of self. More significantly, his unwillingness to disclose his real identity leads him to keep significant others—including his wife—at arm's length. The person who seems to know Frank best is Carl Hanratty (Tom Hanks), a detective who is trying to capture and arrest him. Carl figures out that underneath Frank's veneers is a lonely young man, a revelation that both angers and compels Frank. By story's end, Carl becomes something of a father figure to Frank and helps him reestablish a legitimate identity.

Catch Me If You Can illustrates the costs, rewards, and ethical dilemmas of deception and self-disclosure in interpersonal relationships. One of the many morals to the story is that money and prestige cannot satisfy the basic human need to be known and loved by others.

DINER

Year: 1982
Director: Barry Levinson
Rating: R

Communication Concepts:
Gender
Relational Intimacy
Self-Disclosure

Diner is the story of a group of young men in the late 1950s who hang out with each other at a local diner. All of them have fears about growing up and relating to women. Billy (Daly) has gone away to college but returns for Eddie's (Guttenberg) wedding—and also to try to work things out with an old girlfriend (Dowling) who is pregnant with his child. Eddie is engaged but isn't quite sure why he is getting married. Shrevie (Stern) is married to Beth (Barkin), his high school sweetheart, but their relationship is rocky. Boogie (Rourke) is working his way through law school while holding down a job at a hair salon; he is also deep in debt from gambling. Fenwick (Bacon) may be the smartest of the group, but he is drowning his unhappiness life in booze. The diner is the one thing that remains stable while everything else in their lives is changing. Over food, coffee, and cigarettes, they discuss the "important" matters in life like sex, sports, and rock and roll. While their conversations may seem trivial, the time spent together cements their relationship. The guys have troubles in their lives; they may not understand (and in fact, fear) women; they may not want to grow up; but they have each other—and the diner.

This is a movie that is located in both the comedy and the drama sections of video stores. On the comedy side, it has overtones of *American Graffiti* in its nostalgia and bawdy sense of humor (some of the humor may be deemed inappropriate for the classroom; teacher discretion advised). On the drama side, it has overtones of *Breaking Away* in its coming-of-age themes (in fact, Daniel Stern plays a central character in both films).

In an advanced interpersonal communication course, I juxtapose the movies *Diner* and *Steel Magnolias* to discuss differences in male and female communication patterns. In conjunction with the films, the students read the "Gossip" chapter from Deborah Tannen's *You Just Don't Understand: Women and Men in Conversation* and an article entitled, "In a Different Mode: Masculine Styles of Communicating Closeness" by Julia Wood and Christopher Inman (*Journal of Applied Communication Research,* 1993, Vol. 21, pp. 279–95). The comparison/contrast leads to stimulating class discussions.

FARGO

Year: 1996
Director: Joel Coen
Rating: R

Communication Concepts:
Communication Climate (Confirmation/Disconfirmation)

The friendly people of snowy Minnesota and North Dakota provide an eerily contrasting backdrop for *Fargo*'s story of the unraveling of Jerry Lundegaard (William H. Macy), a seemingly normal car salesperson, husband, and father. His life takes a tragic turn when financial problems and persistent disrespect from his father-in-law, Wade Gustafson (Harve Presnell), lead him to the ill-fated scheme of having his wife kidnapped.

The film depicts a culture where confirming communication is the norm. In particular, police officer Marge Gunderson (Frances McDormand) has an affirming style that differs from the typical depiction of gruff cops in the movies. When her colleague Lou (Bruce Bohne) makes an obvious mistake, Marge gently says "I'm not sure that I agree with you one-hundred percent on your police work." She then tells a joke to lessen the embarrassment of his error. In a scene where Jerry swears and stomps off to get something Marge has asked for, she apologizes rather than responding in anger. Later, Marge catches kidnapper Gaear Grimsrud (Peter Stormare) brutally killing his partner in order to steal his share of the money. After apprehending him, she looks at him with pity and says in a soft voice, "There's more to life than a little money. Don't you know that?"

In contrast, Wade disregards Jerry with a variety of disconfirming messages. Wade uses an impervious response when Jerry approaches him while watching a hockey game on TV. Jerry asks, "Who they playing?" Wade only grunts at the TV, ignoring Jerry completely. At dinner, Wade uses a tangential response when Jerry brings up a business proposal about buying some land and building a parking lot. Wade switches topics to a parking lot he managed decades earlier. Wade then gives an ambiguous response when Jerry tries to steer the topic back by saying, "This could work out great for me and Jean (his wife) and Scotty (his son)." Wade replies, "Jean and Scotty never have to worry," noticeably excluding Jerry in his response. Later in the movie, Wade puts down Jerry with lines such as "You don't know. You're just whistling Dixie here" and "Jerry, I don't want you mucking things up."

Fargo shows that it's possible to use confirming communication even in difficult situations. It also shows how destructive a steady diet of disconfirming communication can be.

FREAKY FRIDAY

Year: 2003
Director: Mark Waters
Rating: PG

Communication Concepts:
Nonverbal Communication
Perception/Empathy

In the tradition of *Big*, *Vice Versa*, and previous versions of *Freaky Friday*, the 2003 adaptation of this movie is about people inhabiting older/younger bodies and learning about lives outside their own. In this case, it's mother Tess Coleman (Jamie Lee Curtis) switching bodies and roles with teenage daughter Annabell (Lindsay Lohan).

Before Tess steps into Annabell's world, she has little empathy for the issues in her daughter's life, such as Annabell's struggles with a classmate who bullies her and a teacher who treats her unfairly. Once Tess spends time in Annabell's shoes, she realizes that she hasn't been listening to or understanding her daughter—and that some of Annabell's "whining" was actually legitimate complaining about unjust treatment. Likewise, when Annabell becomes Tess for a few days, she learns that it's not easy to balance the many responsibilities and demands of adulthood, parenthood, and a career.

One of the easiest ways to remember "who's who" in this identity-switching movie is to watch the characters' nonverbal cues. Although viewers see Tess's body, it's clear that it's being inhabited by a teenage girl if you watch her mannerisms and facial expressions and listen to her vocal tone, rate, and pitch. Similarly, when Tess inhabits her daughter's body, she suddenly engages in a variety of adult behaviors—such as adjusting her teen friend's blouse so it shows less of her midriff (something only a mother would do). Add these nonverbal cues to the ways in which Tess and Annabell talk differently when they assume each other's roles and it's easy to see that communication patterns are basic to a person's individual, social, and group identity.

LOST IN TRANSLATION

Year: 2003
Director: Sofia Coppola
Rating: R

Communication Concepts
Intercultural Communication
Relational Stages
Self-Concept (Reflected Appraisal)
Self-Disclosure

Bob Harris (Bill Murray) is an American actor on location in Tokyo to film a whiskey commercial. Away from his wife and isolated in an unfamiliar culture, he is plagued by sleeplessness and loneliness. Bob is repeatedly frustrated, knowing that he only understands a fraction of what others—including film directors, a prostitute, and talking exercise machines—are conveying to him in Japanese.

Then he meets Charlotte (Scarlett Johnasson), an American woman about half his age. She, too, is lonely because her photographer husband is more interested in his work than in her. Like Bob, Charlotte wanders the streets of Tokyo alone, trying to make sense of the unfamiliar culture while taking stock of her life.

Bob and Charlotte strike up a close friendship, built largely on the respect and trust they develop through self-disclosure. Bob looks at Charlotte wistfully and wonders how he might have built a closer relationship with his own wife. Charlotte looks to Bob for advice about how to remedy her tepid marriage. Bob and Charlotte become powerful sources of reflected appraisal for each other as both try to sort out their identities and how proceed from their own relational crossroads.

Charlotte and Bob quickly reach a platonic intensifying stage as they spend most of their time in Tokyo together, offering each other much needed support. The audience is left wondering whether Bob and Charlotte's relationship will become romantic. In any case, they clearly learn a great deal about themselves and each other as a result of being "strangers in a strange land" together.

SHREK

Year: 2001
Director: Andrew Adamson
Rating: PG

Communication Concepts
Communication Competence
Perception/Stereotyping
Relationships

Shrek is the winsome story of a misunderstood ogre (voice of Mike Myers), a talkative donkey (voice of Eddie Murphy), and a beautiful princess (voice of Cameron Diaz). As is typical of most fairy tales, there are dragons, villains, and a magical ending. At the same time, this animated feature offers some interesting and very "human" communication illustrations.

Of particular interest is the relationship between Shrek and the donkey. Only moments after meeting Shrek, the donkey confides, "I don't have any friends"—and it soon becomes apparent why. The donkey exhibits communicative incompetence at every turn. He makes insulting comments about Shrek's breath and house (then tries to make amends with insincere flattery), offers inappropriate self-disclosures, and refuses to take no for an answer. When an exasperated Shrek says, "It's no wonder you don't have any friends," the donkey cluelessly responds, "Only a true friend would be that cruelly honest." His cluelessness continues when he tells Shrek, "I hate it when you've got somebody in your face and you're trying to give them a hint and they won't leave"—without being aware that he is guilty of that very fault.

So why do Shrek and the donkey ultimately become friends? Over time, Shrek finds that the donkey has redeeming qualities as well as unsavory ones. The donkey is loyal to a fault, persistent in adversity, and doesn't give up on Shrek even though the ogre tries to push him away. Shrek admits later in the story that he shuts others out of his life because he is tired of being stereotyped: "They judge me before they even know me—that's why I'm better off alone." The donkey responds by saying that he didn't judge Shrek when they first met—in fact, he liked Shrek from moment one. A bond develops because the donkey and Shrek each have strengths that the other needs. One moral to the story: initial acts of communicative incompetence aren't necessarily fatal to developing and maintaining successful relationships.

TOOTSIE

Year: 1982
Director: Sydney Pollack
Rating: PG

Communication Concepts
Conflict
Empathy
Gender
Language
Perception

Michael Dorsey (Dustin Hoffman) is a struggling New York actor who waits tables and teaches acting classes. He has a reputation for being difficult to work with; as a result, no one will cast him. Michael resorts to changing his identity to a woman, Dorothy Michaels. He/she lands a part in a daytime soap opera, playing a hospital administrator who is assertive, opinionated, and feminine. Dorothy becomes a star—and a role model for women viewers around the country.

No one knows the truth except Michael's agent George (Sydney Pollack) and roommate Jeff (Bill Murray). He hides his secret from his friend Sandy (Teri Garr), who lost the part to Dorothy, and from fellow soap star Julie (Jessica Lange), with whom he falls in love (and whom Dorothy befriends). Director Ron (Dabney Coleman) despises Dorothy but is romantically involved with Julie. Along the way, Julie's father (Charles Durning) falls for Dorothy, as does another soap actor (George Gaynes). Thus, Michael must juggle a variety of roles and a variety of lies to maintain his job and his sanity.

The situation escalates, and Michael decides he wants to just be himself again. When he reveals his identity on a live broadcast, everyone is shocked. Julie, in particular, is angry about the deception. The story ends with Michael apologizing to her, and they decide to start their relationship again as man and woman. Michael's ruse gives him a new perspective on life. He gains a sense of empathy for women and learns things about himself as a result of playing Dorothy.

Tootsie is an entertaining and popular film that is familiar to many students. In the 1980s, class discussions about *Tootsie* often focused on the accuracy of stereotypes (i.e., women in the class usually argued that Ron's sexism was typical of males, while the men argued that it wasn't). Beginning in the 1990s, class discussions started revolving around issues of sexual harassment (i.e., what would happen if Ron were so blatantly sexist in today's workplace). Both topics make for engaging debates and lively discussions.

A valuable tool to enhance analysis of *Tootsie* is an interview of Dustin Hoffman by Leslie Bennetts, "Tootsie Taught Hoffman About the Sexes" (published in *The New York Times* on December 21, 1982 and available in *The New York Times Biographical Service,* Vol. 13, No. 12, pp. 1631–32). The article describes what Hoffman learned about women and himself through playing the role of Dorothy. He says that Dorothy "made me very emotional," to the point of crying during a screen test. He claims he became "much less impatient, more tolerant of mistakes, particularly my own" as a result of the role. He also discusses prejudices about attractiveness and games between the sexes. The article is a highly recommended example of life imitating art.

SECTION VI
REFERENCES AND RESOURCES

References

Adler, R. B. (1995). Teaching communication theories with *Jungle Fever. Communication Education, 44,* 157–164.

Baker, B. L. (1997). *Using controversial media to teach issues about gender.* ERIC Document ED 416 555.

Baker, B. L., & Lawrence, D. L. (1994). *The effectiveness of using media to teach interpersonal communication: A preliminary study.* ERIC Document 417 437.

Boyatzis, C. J. (1994). Using feature films to teach social development. *Teaching of Psychology, 21,* 99–101.

Caputo, J.S., & Smith, A. (1991). *Film in honors rhetoric: Students' dramaturgical analyses of The Mission.* ERIC Document ED 344 26 0.

Daughton, S.M. (1996). The spiritual power of repetitive form: Steps toward transcendence in *Groundhog Day. Critical Studies in Mass Communication, 13,* 138–154.

English, F.W., & Steffy, B.E. (1997). Using film to teach leadership in educational administration. *Educational Administration Quarterly, 33,* 107-115.

Gregg, V.R. (1995). *Using feature films to promote active learning in the college classroom.* ERIC Document ED 389 367.

Griffin, C. L. (1995). Teaching rhetorical criticism with *Thelma and Louise. Communication Education, 44,* 165–176.

Harrington, K.V., & Griffin, R.W. (1989). Ripley, Burke, Gorman, and friends: Using the film *Aliens* to teach leadership and power. *Organizational Behavior Teaching Review, 14,* 79–86.

Hinck, S. S. (1995). *Integrating media into the communication classroom as an experiential learning tool: A guide to processing and debriefing.* ERIC Document ED 399 573.

Hodak, J.M. (1995). *Children of a Lesser God:* A film for relational study. *Speech Communication Teacher, 9, 3*–4.

Hugenberg, B.S. (2000). Teaching naturalistic inquiry with *Instinct. Communication Teacher, 15,* 10-13.

Jensen, M.D. (1981). *Teaching interpersonal communication through novels, plays, and films.* ERIC Document ED 213 055.

Johnson, S.D., & Iacobucci, C. (1995). Teaching small group communication with *The Dream Team. Communication Education, 44,* 177–182.

Koch, G., & Dollarhide, C.T. (2000). Using popular film in counselor education: *Good Will Hunting* as a teaching tool. *Counselor Education and Supervision, 39,* 203-210.

Leblanc, L. (1998). Using feature films to teach ethnographic methods. *Teaching Sociology, 26,* 62-68.

Long, T. (1998). *Date with an Angel: A non-verbal communication teaching tip.* ERIC Document ED 425 481.

Mackey-Kallis, S., & Kirk-Elfenbein, S. (1997). *A mass-media centered approach to teaching the course in family communication.* ERIC Document ED 439 463.

McGowan, L. (1993). *St. Elmo's Fire* as a tool for discussing conflict management. *Speech Communication Teacher, 7,* 12–13.

McKinney, B. C. (1990). The group process and *12 Angry Men. Speech Communication Teacher, 4,* 1–2.

O'Mara, J. (1991). Teaching intercultural communication through the Hollywood film: An analysis of *Witness.* ERIC Document ED 336 7 65.

Patterson, L. R., & Lindberg, S. W. (1991). *The nature of copyright: A law of users' rights.* Athens, GA: University of Georgia.

Proctor, R. F. (1990). Interpersonal communication and feature films: A marriage worthy of a course. *Michigan Association of Speech Communication Journal, 25,* 1–12.

Proctor, R. F. (1991). Do the ends justify the means? Thinking critically about *Twelve Angry Men.* ERIC Document ED 336 784.

Proctor, R. F. (1991). *Teaching group communication with feature films.* ERIC Document ED 343 175.

Proctor, R. F. (1992). *Roger and Me:* A critique for the classroom. *Journal of the Oklahoma Speech Theatre Communication Association, 14,* 75–78.

Proctor, R. F. (1992). Teaching small group communication with feature films. *Journal of the Illinois Speech Theatre Association, 43,* 28–37.

Proctor, R. F. (1993). *Homework and Network: Applications for communication theory.* ERIC Document ED 359 581.

Proctor, R. F. (1993). Using feature films to teach critical thinking: Multiple morals to the stories. *Speech Communication Teacher, 7,* 11–12.

Proctor, R. F. (1995). Teaching communication courses with feature films: A second look. *Communication Education, 44,* 155–156.

Proctor, R. F. (2000). Using *Swing Kids* to teach theories of persuasion. *Communication Teacher, 14,* 5-6.

Proctor, R. F., & Adler, R. B. (1991). Teaching interpersonal communication with feature films. *Communication Education, 40,* 393–400.

Proctor, R. F., & Johnson, S. D. (1994). *Feature films for communication courses.* ERIC Document ED 364 928.

Proctor, R. F., & Johnson, S. D. (1994). Feature films for communication courses: A bibliography. *Speech and Theatre Association of Missouri Journal, 24,* 71–76.

Proctor, R. F., & Rock, R. (1995). Using *Children of a Lesser God* to teach intercultural communication. ERIC Document ED 386 765.

Proctor, R. F., & Rock, R. (1996). Using *Children of a Lesser God* to teach intercultural communication. *Communication and Theater Association of Minnesota Journal, 23,* 83–89.

Remender, P. A. (1992). Using feature films to encourage critical thinking. *Southern Social Studies Journal, 17,* 33–44.

Roberto, A. J. (1997). Stages of relationships: Examples from *When Harry Met Sally. Speech Communication Teacher, 11,* 10–12.

Safran, S. P. (2000). Using movies to teach students about disabilities. *Teaching Exceptional Children, 32,* 44-47.

Schrader, D. (1997). Media to enhance learning: Using film to teach intercultural communication. *Speech Communication Teacher, 11,* 6–9.

Serey, T. T. (1992). Carpe diem: Lessons about life and management from *Dead Poets Society. Journal of Management Education, 16,* 374–381.

Siddens, P. J. (1992). Literary texts, films, and solo performances. *Speech Communication Teacher, 6,* 7–8.

Siddens, P. J. (2000). Using the feature film *American History X* to teach principles of self-concept in the *Introduction to Interpersonal Communication* course. ERIC Document ED 440 412.

Smitter, R. (1994). *Using feature films to integrate themes and concepts in the basic course.* ERIC Document ED 378 611.

Speere, L., & Parsons, P. (1995). The copyright implications of using video in the classroom. *Journalism Educator, 49,* 11–20.

Summerfield, E. (1993). *Crossing cultures through film.* Yarmouth, ME: Intercultural Press.

Vicek, C. W. (1992). *Adoptable copyright policy: Copyright policy and manuals designed for adoption by schools, colleges, and universities.* ERIC Document ED 364 208.

Winegarden, A. D., Fuss-Reineck, M., & Charron, L. J. (1993). Using *Star Trek: The Next Generation* to teach concepts in persuasion, family communication, and communication ethics. *Communication Education, 42,* 179–188.

Zorn, T. E. (1991). Willy Loman's lesson: Teaching identity management with *Death of a Salesman. Communication Education, 40,* 219–22 4.

Feature Film Websites of Interest

Now Playing Online
www.oup.com/us/playingnow

Film Clips Online
www.filmclipsonline.com

Teach with Movies
www.teachwithmovies.org

Hartwick Classic Film Leadership Cases
http://www.hartwickinstitute.org/Store.aspx?Action=Sort&Type=Film

The Internet Movie Database
www.imdb.com

Film.Com
www.film.com

Movie Review Query Engine
www.mrqe.com

Roger Ebert Print Reviews
rogerebert.suntimes.com

INDEX BY COMMUNICATION CONCEPTS